Answers From Above

Answers From Above

A Handbook for the New Millennium

Alan and Pamela Fass

Aseer Publishing
Washburn, Tennessee
1999

Answers From Above
A Handbook for the New Millennium

Aseer Publishing, P.O. Box 188, Washburn, TN 37888

Published 1999
Printed in the United States of America

05 04 03 02 01 00 99   7 6 5 4 3 2 1

ISBN 0-9661444-5-7

Library of Congress Catalog Card Number: 97-094983

Cover photo: Cades Cove, Great Smoky Mountains National Park
Cover design by Abacus Graphics, Oceanside, California
Hand photography by Alan Muir

Printed on recycled paper with soy-based inks

www.answersfromabove.com

Dedicated to all
who search for answers

With special thanks to
Tony Palmer
and
Mike Budd

For my husband,
the man who gives me
life, love, and answers
I will love you
forever

To my wife
and soulmate, Pamela
Together we have realized our dreams
You make every day worth living
I will love you
forever

Contents

ACKNOWLEDGMENTS

Many people have provided us with advice, assistance, and answers throughout our lives. First and foremost, we must honor the contributions of our parents, Herb and Pat Fass, and Robert and Anne Pevahouse. Without their encouragement and support, we might have followed a path that led us away from the answers. They have always offered us a stable foundation, even when the world seemed to be increasingly unstable.

Our siblings also have contributed greatly to our lives. Dale Fass has always traveled the road not taken and encouraged Alan's explorations into the unknown from the very beginning. Wayne Fass has offered and continues to offer a model of strength, independence, and stability that has inspired Alan to emulate many of his qualities. Debra Fass Hudson has always shown compassion for all people, commitment to her family, and courage in the face of adversity, qualities that offer constant inspiration to others. Laura Fass Muir has challenged all boundaries since childhood and continues to make great strides for herself as well as all women; her strength and determination, tempered with compassion for those less empowered, make her a constant source of inspiration for both of us. Scott and Sherry Pevahouse, while fighting many individual battles, have inspired us to never stop searching for answers, regardless of the difficulties placed before us. And Pat Ladig has taught us that it is okay, and even preferable, that we are all different.

Mike Budd holds a special place in our hearts. His dedication to the written and spoken word is second to few. His indirect help with this manuscript gave us the opportunity to offer these wise words to the world. Although you did not get the official praise (yet), you will have our gratitude for life.

Tony Palmer works quietly, but the impact of his good deeds will be felt by countless souls on this plane and the other. He gives unselfishly, asking for no reward but the betterment of humankind. Without him, *Answers From Above* would never have been written. Our gratitude and respect will be yours forever.

John R. Webster and Francie Droll of Abacus Graphics shared in our vision from the beginning. From an outline of our ideas and a handful of our photographs, they created the perfect cover for our book. Thanks to John's advice and dedication to this project, coupled with his amazing design ability, every element on the cover holds special meaning for us and captures our vision beautifully. Francie used her vast knowledge of typography and design to creatively bring new life to our title, subtitle, spine, and back cover copy. Francie and John's combined exceptional work on the cover will help others to easily see the beauty within.

We also wish to thank Linda Farquhar Lacey for her valuable contributions regarding the design of the book. She helped us to see that simplicity has a greater impact than complexity.

Steve Pate and Becky Allison-Pate of Gilliland Printing offered us much more than a business relationship from the very beginning. They helped two relative newcomers to overcome the numerous challenges of the printing process. We are thankful that we entrusted our work to such competent, compassionate, and committed people.

A special thanks goes to Alan Muir for spending an entire Saturday afternoon painstakingly photographing our hands so that we could achieve the perfect picture for the cover design. Thanks also to Laura Muir for her hand modeling expertise.

We would like to thank Ray Ledbetter, Bob and Anne Pevahouse, Wayne Fass, Linda Farquhar Lacey, Laura and Alan Muir, Kathy McClure, Scot and Heather Wehmeyer, Dan Goin, Agnes Martin, Marci Snow, Adele Dabbs Fraioli, and Dick Hayes for their valuable feedback on the cover design.

So many others have contributed to our lives and our work, whether they are aware of it or not. We would like to thank Sherwell Federlick, Caryn Neumann, Charlie Murray, Rosemary Cathcart, Eva Smimo, Sonia Elcock, Mila Scalise, Adele Dabbs, Sheila Burke, Julie Harnett, Terry Trzepacz, Bette Beardsley, James Schaller, Anita Meier, Ann Karda, James Hudson, Sue Fass, Ted Brown, Myrtle Pevahouse, O.W.B. Brown, Stephen Anderson, John Martinuzzi, Ramsey Pevsner, Harriet Margolis, Karen

Davis, Glenn Singer, Sam Zagoria, David Nixon, Mary Faraci, Charles Finkl, Richard Yinger, Helen Bannan, Barbara Matthews, Eleanor Salisbury, Heather Frazer, Lynn Appleton, Becky Mulvaney, Art Evans, Fred Fejes, Dorothy Stetson, Norman Nathan, Michael Miles, Dan Hahn, Voncile Smith, Elaine Stern, Fritz Postlewaithe, Avel Abrams, Freda Fell, Shri Bodhisattva, members of the Aquarian Research Center, and June Bales (for providing our workplace).

We give special thanks to Kristy Graham and Joey Pevahouse; Emily Smith; Brieta, Amy, and Shelley Fass; Stephanie, Tara, Jimmy, and Bradley Hudson; Rex Jr., Alex, and Alina; and the spirits of Autumn and Asepf. These special people remind us every day why it is so important to find the answers.

We would also like to thank some people that we have never met but who have helped and inspired us tremendously through their written works: Sanaya Roman and Duane Packer, Edgar Cayce, James Redfield, Louise L. Hay, Shakti Gawain, Raymond A. Moody, Jr., Mary Summer Rain, Shirley MacLaine, Richard Bach, Anthony de Mello, Jack Canfield and Mark Victor Hansen, Harold Kushner, Wayne Dyer, Betty J. Eadie, Dannion Brinkley, Sue Patton Thoele, Jerrold R. Jenkins and Mardi Link, Dan Poynter, Avery Cardoza, Robin Williams, Ted Alspach, Nigel French, the Maran family, Sean Cavanaugh, Amy Dacyczyn, Don Aslett, Mark Beach, Tom and Marilyn Ross, Robert Lawrence Holt, Jonathan Kirsch, Robert C. Pinckert, and William Zinsser. We hope our contribution will be as beneficial to others as yours have been.

A special thanks to my best friend, Helaine Fuchsman, for always providing friendship, support, and encouragement, especially when life has led me down challenging and difficult roads. You have provided me with an extended family, given me shelter until the storms subside, and offered me hope when the light in my heart grew dim. It is the numerous, unselfish acts of others that lead to our own great accomplishments.

And we thank those earthbound and spiritual beings who have always encouraged us to search for answers.

Preface

All of my life I have been looking for answers. I learned to read at the age of four. As a child, I spent summers indoors reading the numerous books I had convinced my parents to buy from the school book clubs. As a teenager, I read titles chosen by my teachers. As an adult, just completing my first semester of college, I decided the answers had to be found outside of books. I ventured outward to discover the real meaning of life.

After years of gaining "real world" experience, I began college for the second time at age twenty-eight. Again, I succumbed to the allure of the written word. This time, I chose the titles. My voracious appetite for life's answers was partly satisfied and partly titillated by my college experience.

I have always known there had to be more to our lives than creation, a limited sixty-year-plus existence, and our popular conception of death. After experiencing a personal tragedy that caused me to question the meaning of my life as well as the idea of a universal design or destiny, I spent nine years studying—through books, classes, meditation, and seminars—what has since been described as "New Age" ideas. And then Alan came into my life.

My initial response to channeling was strong skepticism. Is there another dimension of information and can a human actually converse with beings from beyond this world? And why does Alan have access to a dimension that only exists in my imagination? If we can converse with the other side, why don't we all have this ability?

I first began to believe that Alan's channeled messages were authentic after I read some of his college papers and reports from his environmental consulting work. Alan has a great grasp of scientific concepts and writes in a very detail-oriented style. The channeled information was written in a completely different style—simplistic words describing profound concepts—and bore no resemblance to Alan's writing.

As a geology student, Alan had only taken two basic writing courses in college. His academic training did not provide the kind of intense writing experiences that I had come to take for granted. While he is a competent writer on his own, the channeled messages provided a depth and stylistic perfection that I had not achieved during my six years of rigorous instruction in the communication field. So where was this information coming from?

Alan says that he receives messages from two of his spirit guides (angels), Asmuth and Shamani. Exactly how he receives the information is a mystery to me. After "hearing" the answers to hundreds of my questions, though, I have come to realize that I would rather spend my time studying the channeled messages than trying to validate the method of communication. Regardless of the source, these profound words offer answers for anyone willing to listen.

Asmuth and Shamani have given us the answers to hundreds of questions, enough to fill the pages of many books. Some of the messages initially surprised us, partly because of their simplicity, but all of the answers ultimately assuaged our fears and doubts about the unknown. Asmuth and Shamani remind us every day that all problems can be solved with unconditional love.

In chapter one, Asmuth and Shamani point out the contributions and importance of all beings, human and non-human. In chapter two, they help us to discover our inner needs and encourage our self-improvement. In chapter three, they offer alternatives to traditional notions about healthcare; ultimately, we are the masters of our own bodies. In chapter four, they remind us that we are loving beings and invite us to open up to the possibilities of love.

Chapter five explores the depths of our sexuality and reminds us how beautiful our physical oneness can be. Chapter six helps us to understand the dynamics of our modern family life and invites us to embrace our children and our parents with love. Chapter seven provides an alternative definition of success for those questioning their current career choices. Chapter eight acknowledges that life is constantly changing and guides us through all of life's stages.

Chapter nine delves into the mysteries about who we are as personal and social beings. Chapter ten presents suggestions as to how we can deal with the vast changes in our world. Chapter eleven challenges readers to look for answers to questions that often seem unanswerable (or that only provide narrow answers). Chapter twelve begins to explore the spiritual side of human life. Chapter thirteen elevates the reader to heights heretofore beyond one's reach. Chapter fourteen offers hope for us, individually and collectively.

Answers From Above tries to offer something for every reader. I know that I have finally found the answers to many of the questions that I began to ask almost forty years ago. I hope that you find the answers to some of your questions as well. And, regardless of your beliefs about the origin of the information, if you are willing to search beyond your present awareness for the answers, amazingly, you will discover that they were hiding inside of you all the time.

Pamela Pevahouse Fass

A Note From Alan

From the point of my soul's conception eons ago as well as in this lifetime, I have searched for answers to life's most intriguing questions. Of all the questions I have asked throughout my many lifetimes, the one I have yet to answer, and the one most important to me, is "Why am I here?" I have journeyed throughout the universe to find the answer to this one question.

As we approach the new decade, the new century, and the new millennium, many of us have begun to question our own existence, our immortality. We come to earth by free choice, and our journey for the truth begins. We each travel a different path but we all take part in the search. I like to think of life's journey as a series of plane flights. We take off from a known place and land at a known destination most of the time. But sometimes we have to take a detour or two to get where we need to be. We question why we need to be challenged so favorably or harshly. Our ultimate goal is to find our truth, our answers.

I have always believed in the existence of angels. As a child, lying in my bed at night, I would see and talk to them. Even though others denied their immediate existence, I have felt their presence throughout my life. During my adolescent years I began to develop an interest in astrology and the worlds beyond the Earth. As an adult, I started on a path of self-discovery with the help of a friend and my soulmate. I immersed myself in metaphysical studies and soon discovered many others voicing similar thoughts and ideas. Then my childhood memories began to emerge.

During a meditation exercise in 1988, I received a vision of an elderly man dressed in flowing white robes, with long white hair and a white beard. This was the first level of contact with my guardian angel (spirit guide), Asmuth, one of the spiritual sources for this book. Later in 1988, I received a vision of a Native American shaman, later to be known as Shamani, the other spiritual source for the book.

For the next seven years, the angels remained nameless and speechless, for I was unknowingly (on a subconscious level) preparing to advance to the second level of contact—communication. I studied Reiki (a form of hands-on healing) under a Reiki Master, psychic medium, and healer who taught me to search within and listen to my inner voice. I meditated daily, opened my mind to other levels of consciousness, and established a connection. As I found my voice, I also found the voices of Asmuth and Shamani.

Now I communicate daily with Asmuth, Shamani, and other guardian angels (spirit guides) to continue to gather the answers from above, answers based on unconditional love—the love that lies within each of our hearts. The questions we ask contain the answers we seek. Ask the questions and listen for the answers—that is the key to life.

We each follow a different path to enlightenment, but goodness awaits all of us. All life is interconnected. I am a time traveler and so are you. If our flights take us to the same destination, let us greet each other with kindness, respect, and love. We all must follow our own path to personal enlightenment.

Within this book you will find the answers to many of your questions. Some answers lie on a predetermined page while others are buried deep within, awaiting your discovery. Do not be afraid of what you might discover. Every question has an answer. Life on earth is a series of questions awaiting the answers.

As we move into the new millennium, we will have many questions that need to be answered. Pamela and I will continue to ask the questions, and Asmuth and Shamani will continue to provide the answers, until we have all found the answers that we need. Ultimately, we shall all answer the most important question, "Why am I here?"

Begin the search if you haven't already. Place this book in your hand and listen with your heart.

Alan J. Fass

Part I:
Introduction

Chapter 1:
Answers About the World Around Us

Both ancient and modern wisdom is contained within the pages of this chapter. The sparrow sings a song for each of you. Are you ready to hear what it has to say? Nature is all around you, it is the basis of life. Covet thy soul with the sounds of nature: raindrops falling gently on a leaf, the leaves rustling in the wind, the insects singing to each other, the wolf howling at the night sky, and the eagle flapping its wings in prayer. What song do you hear in your heart, when you think of these sounds?

The insects, animals, trees, rocks, sand, and lakes and oceans may not speak in a human voice, but each has a voice nonetheless. And if you open your mind and heart, you too can hear their voices. Oh precious Earth, that which gives you life. Simple yet complex enough to sustain an infinite amount of creatures, "living" and "non-living." Yes, you are one of these creatures. So, take responsibility for what you consume and produce, seek a balance between these two. For if you do, you will see that the world around you will provide you with an infinite source of knowledge and wisdom.

As you read each question, remember that truly the answers lie within you. After you have read the answer, think about how your life can change for the better. You can learn so much from a grain of sand, a rock, and a mountain. But in order to reach the mountain and truly recognize and understand its beauty, you must first ask yourself, "What can I learn from a grain of sand?" (Shamani)

What can we learn from a grain of sand?

A grain of sand is symbolic of the importance of one. One is everything and everything is one. If you have trouble understanding this concept, think of the universe. There is one universe which contains everything. But, everything collectively defines the universe.

A grain of sand is a universe unto itself. If you look at a grain of sand and put it under a magnifier or a microscope, you will see much more than you can with your naked eye. Each grain of sand has individual characteristics of shape, size, translucence, transparence, color, weight, and composition. No two grains of sand are alike, just as no two people or souls are alike. You could spend a lifetime studying one grain of sand.

Some grains of sand are more than a billion years old. Think of a billion years of wisdom and knowledge contained in one grain of sand. If only the grain of sand could speak to you, what would it say? Would you live your life differently?

A grain of sand teaches you that beauty can be found in one thing. A separate universe of wisdom and knowledge can be found in one thing. You are a universe unto yourself. Now, I ask you to explore your own universe and find beauty and love in yourself. Remember, the universe is limitless. (Shamani)

What are our most important personal concerns at this time?

Cathedrals of the heart, you build a monument to yourself. The trees stand individually in the forest. Each tree must sustain itself by utilizing the resources available to it. The air and the land provide nutrients for the tree. The tree coexists in balance with the air and the land. So I say, it is the same with you (humans). Learn to coexist with the land, air, and water. As individuals, it is your personal responsibility to live in balance with the earth. The earth will provide all the nutrients you need.

In order to be in balance with the earth, you must first be in balance with yourself. Balance yourself in mind, body, and spirit.

The body cannot survive without the mind and spirit, and vice versa.

It is up to each and every one of you to find balance. Many can lead you to it, but only you, the individual, can choose it.

As I have said, your most important personal concern is the balance of your mind, body, and spirit. When you achieve this balance, you are like the tree standing in the forest. The tree stands still on its own, plants its roots firmly, and allows the wind to flow naturally through its leaves. (Asmuth)

What can we learn from the trees?

Trees, the keepers of knowledge and eternal wisdom. Look at the tree, standing tall and majestic in the forest. Like you, it grows from a seedling, reaching for the sky to achieve new heights. It branches out, feeling the air rushing between its leaves. It is free and so are you.

Although, it stands tall and firm like a statue in the wind. It sways and rocks, content in knowing that should it fall, the wind shall catch it. The wind is the great protector. So like the tree, be free. Let the wind rush between your fingers, and stand tall and firm. (Shamani)

Trees, the givers of life, full of fruits, nourishment for the body and soul. Bearers of fruit, new ideas, new concepts—this is what you can learn. Listen to the tree, it tells a story. It is a book, a book to be opened. You may think me crazy, but I tell you, many trees have spoken to me. Stand still and listen to the leaves rustling, the trunk swaying and creaking. Most trees have been on earth longer than people. See how they stand the test of time. (Asmuth)

What can we learn from the flowers?

The flowers, a rainbow of colors glistening in the sunlight. The sun shines down upon them, bringing a renewed sense of life. They reach for the sun to show their brilliance and beauty.

Flowers, they are for you to enjoy. A gift from the heart, a symbol of my love for you.

Place a flower in your hand, caress it, feel its softness. Run the petals through your fingers.

Smell the flowers, the essence (scent) of each one is different.

Look at the flowers, they are a symbol of spirit personified.

So I say to you, take time to touch, smell, and see the flowers. You have the gift of touch, smell, and sight—learn to appreciate these gifts.

In a flower, I can see love. It is not the physical appearance itself, but the essence of the flower. The flowers can teach you that there is beauty and love in everyone and everything, if you are willing to look beneath the surface. (Shamani)

What can we learn from the sunflower?

Oh flower of brilliant radiance, it reaches out to capture the sun. From one sunflower comes many seeds, nourishment for the birds, insects, and humans.

If you look closely, you can see the face of the sun in the sunflower. Petals of yellow and leaves of green, from a seed these were born. The thousands of seeds in one sunflower are symbolic of a human's thoughts and feelings. From one seed (you), a thousand thoughts and feelings are created.

Like the fruit inside the sunflower seed, your thoughts and feelings are encased in a shell. Only until you open the shell can you see what truly lies within each thought and feeling.

Each of you represents a seed in a garden of paradise. Each of you will grow at your own rate. You are like sunflowers. Some of you have blossomed into flowers, while others are still growing. Remember that each of you has the ability to blossom into flowers and bear fruit.

Just as each seed in the sunflower can create a new life, so too can each of your thoughts and feelings create a new life. Even if the seed never falls to the ground and develops into a plant, the seed still provides life for the bird or insect that eats it. Furthermore, if the bird or insect reproduces, the life energy of the sunflower seed will live on in the next generation of birds or insects.

The same is with your thoughts and feelings. The seeds you plant provide nourishment for others. The energy in each thought and feeling can be passed on for several generations. Also, remember that thoughts and feelings can be positive or negative. And so, you must be careful to plant only the seeds of love.

The garden of wisdom has many plants in it. Each plant or flower can teach you something. Open yourself like the sunflower and receive the light. (Asmuth)

Where do rainbows come from?

The Roman soldiers prepare for battle. What stories will they later tell? Will it be stories of bloodshed, or hope and love? This is where the rainbows of love begin.

See the many colors of the rainbow, those you can see and those you can not see. The color purple emanates brilliantly from the rainbow. What does the color purple symbolize? Why, healing of course. And are you not filled with love and joy when you see a rainbow? The love and joy you feel is part of you, you are a symbol of beauty. You are a rainbow in disguise.

You see a rainbow most often in the sky, although sometimes you may see it in a crystal. So you ask, where do rainbows come from? Nature, the greatest provider of what you've come to know as beauty. What is nature but the embodiment of love and peace. See the doves which fly in the sky. When you see two doves, does this not remind you of love? Love is the union of all things, "living" and "non-living." Nature is the provider and caretaker of all things.

So you see, the rainbow is an extension of nature's love for you. A rainbow is a true expression of beauty and love. Remember that you are a symbol of beauty and love too. If you let your colors shine through, others will see you as a rainbow of love and peace. Let your true colors shine through, you will soon see how beautiful you really are. Then you will no longer need to look outside yourself to recognize beauty. (Asmuth)

What do we get from the color yellow?

The leaves of gold shine upon you to show you the path. The path to the truth is lined with goldenrod (flowers).

The sun bursts out of the nighttime sky in such dramatic fashion. Rising above the horizon to greet you, heralding the start of a new day. The new day awakens new visions in you who are ready to receive them. The visions you receive may not always be profound but they are nonetheless important.

The truth can be found in any color. Do you see color as just a color—something intangible? Well, I tell you, you can see, hear, feel, taste, and smell color. Many of you may think this is impossible. But I say that you do not know color. For until you have embraced all that color is, you do not know color.

So I say, do not limit your perception to the surface of things. If you go through life only seeing color in every person, place, or thing, what will you truly learn? You will only recognize and categorize everything in your world on what you see on the surface. There is so much that lies beneath the surface. Color is only a coating, used to enhance the vibrational energy of the object which wears it.

Do you often judge others (people, places, or things) by the color of their skin or what they wear? Do you criticize others based on their color? Do you love others because they share the same color? Remember that color is only skin deep.

I ask you to look beyond the color and coating of all things of creation. Beneath the surface of everyone and everything lies a soul. The soul is colorless but you can recognize it in each other, if you only open your eyes. Look up and see that the golden leaves shine upon you to show you the path. (Shamani)

What do we get from the color green?

You see the color green every day, in your actions, thoughts, and feelings. The color green is a part of the landscape. See the plants and trees, such a colorful green.

Many of you are green with envy, envious of what another person, place, or thing has. I see many of you flashing green pieces of paper at each other. You attach much significance to this color, it seems to be the basis of your society. But I ask you to think of this—if you were born in darkness and never saw the color green, what significance would it have? Would battles of will and wars of ego be prevalent on the earth plane?

There is much beauty in the plants and trees. There are an infinite number of shades of green. But it is not the color green that is important. Green is just your perception of color and the importance you assign to it.

What does the object which you perceive as green embody? The answer is spirit, the essence of life. The trees and plants breathe so that you and all life on Earth may live. Now, do you see why the color green is so important? If you choose money and greed over plants and trees, you will soon be green with envy, envious of the life you do not have. (Shamani)

Where did the mountains come from?

The mountains were conceived from the light and in the light, as well as all things of creation. From the light was born a universe. The universe gave "birth" to a child which you know as Earth. The Earth is an entity unto itself. Unto the Earth, you were born. So the same is with the mountains. Many before you have created myths and legends about where the mountains came from. Many of you still argue about the origin of the mountains.

Now I will tell you. The Earth is a "living" being, not in the traditional sense of life as you know and express it. It is a creation by which no other thing can be measured. Think of the earth as a glowing ember, radiating energy outward. Think of the core of the earth as its soul. All light radiates from the soul. The essence of the Earth can be found in its soul. It is from its soul that the mountains were born.

You see the mountains as being the highest points on earth. The mountains reach into the sky like the fingers of a child. A symbol of strength, can their enormous presence also be a symbol of beauty? Their counterparts, the oceans, seemingly the lowest points on earth, are also a symbol of strength and beauty. Could the mountains and oceans have manifested themselves, devoid of the Earth's soul? So I ask you to recognize that your soul is the core of your being. Reach for the highest and lowest points of yourself, and bring both into the middle, the core of your being. See the Earth as you do yourself, a creation by which no other thing can be measured. (Shamani)

Why do we have night and day?

Why do we have life and death? Throughout the universe, there are contrasts. Light, circles of light and darkness.

Some live by night, others live by day. Daylight brings the joy of a new day. Light helps the plants and animals grow.

Think if you never saw the sunrise or never saw the full moon. Both sun and moon, radiantly glowing, awakening our souls.

Why is there black and white? Think if there were no contrasts, if everything were the same. Would we learn at the same rate?

Differences bring people together. Are you not always seeking something different: a new idea, a new emotion, a new thought? The differences are our own perceptions, just as the perception of night and day is different for everyone. (Asmuth)

Why do the seasons change?

Change is ever present, nothing stays the same. So too it is with the seasons. On earth, the seasons change, from winter comes rebirth into spring. Summer is abundant with life and then to autumn, a time of change. It is a complete cycle of life for some creatures. For other creatures, each season is a time of renewal.

Think of the polar bear, it relishes the return of winter. It thrives in the cold whereas other creatures die or seek shelter. Each creature lives or dies by the season.

The seasons change as a tribute to the earth, for the earth, and of the earth. The earth consists of cycles, and the earth itself rotates within the universal cycle.

The four seasons on earth symbolize the four stages of human life. Your life begins in the spring as a seed in the ground. You emerge from the ground and grow as a child. Once you reach the summer of your life, you are a young adult, much like the leaves on a tree. You do much of your growth during this period. You will have to weather many storms during this period. This will be a test of survival. The third quarter of your life is like autumn. The leaves on the tree begin to change colors and the tree must shed its leaves in order to survive. The same is true for you, you begin to change, the old ideas don't work anymore, you must change in order to survive. As winter draws near, so does the end of your life. But there is peace and solitude in the forest after a fresh blanket of snow has fallen. This is what awaits you.

So you see, if the seasons did not change, there would be no birth, no death, and no rebirth. The birds, butterflies, frogs, plants, animals, and insects would be gone forever. And soon you would be gone, for your life is dependent on them.

May the seasons of your life be filled with spontaneity, love, grace, and purpose. (Shamani)

What can we learn from the snow?

Snow, a symbol of purity. A soft blanket of white covers the landscape. The ground you saw yesterday is but a distant memory today. Do you know what truly lies beneath what you can not see? Think of the snow as white feathers which caress and cover the ground. What is snow but a protective cover for the earth.

In the spring, the snow melts and provides water for many of you to drink. Think of the mountains as huge reservoirs of water waiting to be tapped. But conserve the water you have, frivolous use only denies your fellow beings the benefit of water. Count your blessings if you have an abundance of water, for those in arid climates can only hope that the skies shall open and drop rain.

A freshly laid blanket of snow is always a welcome sight. It may cause you inconvenience but think of the inconvenience of having no water to drink or bathe with. Enjoy the snow if you live in a cold climate. It is nice to look at and play in.

Remember, snow gives life to the landscape and you. Learn to live with it, as it has learned to live with you. The best gift you can give to the earth is love and respect for all things. The earth provides you with an environment which you can survive in. Accept the gifts the earth has given you, namely the snow. Without the snow, you may never be able to recognize the simplicity and purity of all things, living and non-living. (Shamani)

What relationship should we have with the animals?

Coexistence is the key, walk hand in hand with them. They are sacred beings, beings born of the light, as you are. They understand the language of the trees. Animals harbor no resentment, they understand and trust the natural flow of life. Learn from the animals how to coexist. Learn self-preservation, it is the way of the land. Land for all to inhabit.

Certain animals are symbols for you. Some are revered more than others. But I say to you, if you revere one, revere the other. The falcon is no more important than the killer whale. Each has its place in the order of things. The order of things is that which you call nature.

Natural selection is a way of weeding out that which doesn't work (which isn't working), that which resists the natural flow. Human selection is quite another story, choosing what you think doesn't work. It is not your decision, the natural flow is interrupted. Dam the rivers and you kill the fish. This you know already, but I tire telling it over and over. It falls on deaf ears.

All my relations. Brothers and sisters, we are one. One born in the spirit. (Shamani)

What relationships do animals have with us?

Lighthouses of gold, beacons of light. The light we shine down upon thee. Rivers of gold, ascension by will. Feathers of gold.

Purple pyramids, healing light—the light surrounds us. We are safe, we are well-protected.

Blue earth and sky—the mystery awaits us. Clothe yourself in loincloth.

The whale, majestic in size, is keeper of the deep.

Recognize the beauty of all creatures. Life is interwoven. Even the insects in the grass are part of the circle of life. Life takes many forms, it is not up to you to decide which is right. (Asmuth)

What can we learn from the insects?

The insects, seemingly insignificant and primitive, but I say they are most important. They are very important creatures which are necessary for your survival. On earth, there is a reason and purpose for every life. Divine order is a most efficient system. All life depends on other life. The magic of being is present in every thing. Being is life, life has many forms. It encompasses all that you term "living" and "non-living." There are no coincidences or accidents, there is only life. Life is as it is meant to be. All that is and will ever be is life. Many of you may deny these words and see them as a fabrication. I say to you, can you disprove what I say? There is truth in all I say, if only you look beneath the words. Do the insects question the truth?

The insects are an advanced form of life. They incorporate a communication network which is far superior to human communication. Think of the lifespan of an insect, it seems so short. Indeed it is in your eyes, but look at how much an insect can accomplish. Look at an ant colony—there is an entire system devoted to a purpose. All of the ants work as a unit for the good of all. The ant carries many times its weight. Can the same be said for other animals? I only illustrate differences and attribute superiority to certain things for your understanding and knowledge. I feel I must remind you that all things are equal. I only try to help you understand the concept of universal equality through these examples.

The insects perform the tasks they are best suited for, just as humans do. The whole earth plane is based on a system of cooperation. Everything has a purpose, and in purpose there is everything.

See the insects as creatures that you can learn from. Take notice of their methods of communication and attentiveness to purpose. Remember that learning can be attained on any level, there are no boundaries to learning. Even the smallest creature on the earth can teach you, if you only open your mind. The thought transferred from that insect to you may be the most profound thought in the universe.

Remember that all things have a spirit (soul). Together, we are all one bound by the magic of love. Love all things and in all things you shall find love. (Asmuth)

What can we learn from the birds?

Birds, believers-in-flight. The winged ones travel great distances. Always moving, ever changing, bringing life to the forest.

Learn the call of the bird, the honest uninhibited call of the wild. Let the wild essence of yourself take flight. Go in search of the hidden truths, uncover stones just as the bird does to find worms. It is beneath the stones that the truth lies.

The bird flies high above the earth, encircling its prey. You, the bird of prey, strike down upon your prey and seize the moment.

Your birds—the space shuttles—are birds of prey, going out into space to seek and destroy. Those who want to fly to other galaxies, I say, why aren't you there? You have the power and the means. Play with the toys, the weapons of destruction. The birds of prey fall mightily.

The doves of peace, a symbol to all who seek it. (Shamani)

What can we learn from the sky?

Sacred sky, keeper of ancient secrets and wisdom. The sky is as endless as your mind. An unimaginable number of breaths of air puffed into the sky from everything that has ever lived on earth. The countless thoughts and ideas which float along the ethers, waiting for someone or something to bring them to life again.

The breaths of a million warriors, their lives stood in peril. The wars may be over but the memories are etched in the sky.

Have you ever tried to reach up and touch the sky? Ah, it seems endless and impossible to touch. The sky is ever elusive, what is there to touch but air and a perceived color (blue, white, gray, or black).

The sky is a symbol of life without end and your unlimited potential to love. Love is as endless and dimensionless as the sky. Many of you put dimensions and limits on the sky in a system of three. By this I refer to the idea of three dimensions. There are more dimensions than you perceive. And so, love is not finite and can not be placed in a box. Love defies definition, for it is all that is.

The sky is ever changing from day to night, sunrise to sunset, sunny to cloudy, blue to orange to white, and foggy to clear. The changing sky is much like your emotions. Yet in everything, there is purpose and balance. Although today may be a dismal day, tomorrow may be brighter.

Just as you, the sky can use many disguises. But there is no disguise for the spirit (the soul). The spirit of the sky and everything on earth radiates in all its splendor.

Watch as I drop a feather from the sky. If you see the feather as just a feather of length, width, and height, you only see the limits of your perception. I ask you to watch as the feather floats effortlessly through the air. Catch the feather in your hand, place it between your fingers. See it, touch it, taste it, and become one with it. Once you are one with it, you will know the secrets of the sacred sky.

And so I ask you, do not confine your spirit to the sky. Allow your spirit to soar. May the breaths of all souls, past and present, support your flight. Think about all that I have said, for the secrets and wisdom of the sacred sky can be found in these words. (Shamani)

Part II:
Answers Just for You

Chapter 2:
Answers to Help You Grow

What is life, but a mystery or puzzle? Some of the pieces seem to be missing and others don't seem to fit at all. You were born into this life with a certain amount of knowledge and wisdom. Think of this as a foundation of truth on which you have the opportunity to create your own magic. Think of yourself as a magician, you have the power of illusion and fantasy. But, if you live your life through another person or through illusions or fantasies, you will never grow.

Personal growth is essential to your health, love, sexuality, family, career and success, community, world, universe, spirituality, and everything beyond. There are no limits to your growth, our growth. We are all individuals on different but similar life paths. No one life path is more important than another, we are all equal. However, it is important for each of us to respect and love ourselves and one another.

Your life may seem like a twisted and jumbled experience in complexity and difficulty. But, be assured that no matter how complex or difficult your life may seem, there is growth and purpose in everything. Sometimes, our most difficult lessons are the ones we resist the most. Resistance and growth often stand side by side, waiting to be challenged by the truth. The truth often brings you back into balance, after a period of immense growth or resistance.

From the day you were conceived, you started growing physically, mentally, spiritually, and emotionally. When you were in your mother's womb, all your personal needs were taken care of. But, when you took your first breath of air, you learned that you were on your own now. And from that point on, you have developed into who you are now. You may not be sure about who you are or what you are doing here on Earth. But, rest assured, you have a purpose. It is up to you to develop your own self-identity by challenging yourself to grow as well as others.

Each of you has chosen a path and a method by which to live. So, go forth now and read the words by which your soul lives. As you read this chapter, I ask you to use the words I give you as tools for love and understanding. Always remember that you are the ruler of your destiny and you have all the tools you need to fulfill your life's purpose. You will always grow, even in times when you feel that life has passed you by. I wish you luck and good fortune on your spiritual journey. The greatest lessons in growth can be found in the simplest things in life. Open your body, mind, and soul and raise your level of awareness, personal growth awaits you. (Asmuth)

How can we find joy in our lives?

You can find joy in watching an insect on the ground or by looking at a star in the nighttime sky. Joy is unlimited, you can have as much or as little as you like.

Joy can be found in listening to music, reading a book, speaking to a friend, or just being by yourself. Do you not experience feelings of joy every day?

Joy can be found in simplicity. The simple things in life can be the most enjoyable. The key is to slow down and recognize the beauty around you. What is accomplished by rushing through the day, only to get to tomorrow.

If you can't find joy in your everyday life, what makes you think the future will be any different. Enjoy the present moment, take time to think and contemplate.

If you want to find joy in your life, do something that you really like. Do not deny yourself the pleasure. This can be reading a book or going outdoors and exercising. Watching a butterfly can be the most enriching experience.

Joy comes in large and small packages. Do not limit yourself to the amount of joy you can have. You deserve this and more. (Asmuth)

Why are we given difficult tests?

Difficulty is in the eye of the beholder. You find it difficult to fly but the birds do not. The lesson here is to use what tools you are given in this life.

Some of your life's most difficult lessons are the most important. But you have all the tools you need to complete the task.

For some, love is the most difficult test of a lifetime.

In everything, there is a teacher. Sometimes, you are the teacher and other times, you are the student. When you have learned your lesson, then you become the teacher.

Life is not graded from easy to difficult. It is what you make it. If you wish to have difficult tests, then you shall have them. If you ask for guidance and open yourself to be helped, then the task at hand will not be so difficult. It all lies in your approach. Approach your lessons with love and they will seem easy. (Asmuth)

How can we bolster our self-esteem?

I tell you, see value in everything you do. You are good, affirm it in yourself. Do not let others rule your destiny. For you are the teacher, the teacher of many souls. See value in that.

Heart of gold, this describes you. You are rich, you have the wealth of wisdom. No one can put a price on that. Think of yourself as equal, no one has no more, no less than you. You are divine.

Affirm life, take it by the hand and become one with it. Integrate all life's lessons, the lessons you have chosen. You can learn something from everyone. There are no chance meetings or encounters. Treat everyone with dignity and respect but also realize that you deserve the same. You deserve the best.

If you live near the mountains, try this exercise. Go to the mountains, choose a trail that you would like to walk on. While walking, look up at the leaves on the tree above. Each leaf is beautiful and together the beauty is amplified an infinite amount of times. If several leaves were missing, the tree would appear empty in some places, like a hole. So you see, you are an individual leaf and all your fellow beings are leaves too. Together, we are beautiful and if one of us falls, then a hole is created. A sense of emptiness prevails.

What I say to you is stand up and be counted! Value yourself, love yourself, and be kind to yourself. All of my love I bestow upon you. (Asmuth)

Why do so many people seek the answers from without?

Fear is the driving force, often you are afraid of what you might see if you look inward. It is far easier, you think, to look outside yourself for the answers. But I say you must look within, for until you face yourself you will never resolve the problems or questions you ponder.

Many people are not secure with their own identity. Your identity wears a mask. You ask, is it safe to take off the mask? I say, why do you wear a mask? Are you afraid of what lies beneath the mask or are you afraid of how others might judge you? Security can not be bought, you must develop your own sense of security. Nothing can hurt you unless you allow it to.

People cross bridges to find out what's on the other side. You think the flowers are taller and more beautiful on the other side. You look outside yourself believing that true happiness and love can be found. You build bridges outside yourself. You build monuments and statues to glorify other people or other things.

Do you have any sense of self-preservation? You give away all your energy to other people or things. You believe in doing so, so that you will become a better person. Until you've spent a day alone with yourself in solitude, you really don't know yourself. And when you don't know who you are, what you are doing, and why you are doing it, you will continue to seek the answers from without.

It is good for you to seek help from others when necessary. Learn to trust your intuition. Move forward with individual purpose and intent. A gold mine of information and guidance lies inside you. Look within and you shall find the answers. (Asmuth)

Why do so many of us devalue ourselves and our contributions?

Roses are beautiful, are they not? There are many varieties of roses—red, white, yellow, orange, blue—in all shapes and sizes. Is any one rose prettier than the other? No. Different roses appeal to different people. You may think you are less pretty (physically, mentally, or spiritually) than someone else. But I tell you, you are not.

You have a major contribution to make. Every action in your life has an effect on someone's life. Life is a sacred mystery, there are many twists and turns that we take.

We often don't realize what we have and what we have to offer. We are blinded by our own self-doubt. We are often the most critical of ourselves. We don't give ourselves enough credit, give yourself a pat on the back. You deserve it!

Some of us lack self-esteem. When we don't think highly of ourselves, we fall into a rut. Sometimes, that rut gives us a sense of false security. Security comes from within, feel good about yourself.

Remember you are loved dearly, you are a good person, and you have much to contribute. Remember my analogy of the blocks in the pyramid. Each block is important. If one block is missing, the entire pyramid is affected.

So I say, you may not see value in what you are doing or you may feel that your contributions are worthless. But the truth is that you are a valuable and worthy person. (Asmuth)

How do we learn to value others?

By valuing ourselves. See value in everything you do. You know who you are and what you've become, see value in that. Do not let others wave their wand and cast a spell over you. You are strong and vigilant.

You have a lot to be proud of. Look how far you have come in your life. Stand firm on your principles. You have built a statue of which your principles are a part. Let no hammer or sword come between you and the statue. Your statue is built on truth.

Let no one cast it aside. If you see value in your principles and truth, then you can begin to value others. When you look at someone, perceive their strengths and weaknesses. If you feel so guided, help them to see their strengths and weaknesses. Realize that there is value in both.

Value the ideas of beauty and love. Embrace the spirit of beauty and love. The truth comes to those who seek it. So many value things more than people. So many are wrapped up in the illusion of happiness. Happiness can not be found in things, it must originate within you. So I say, see value in yourself and each other. There can be no greater gift than love. (Asmuth)

How can we accelerate the move toward our true path?

If you listen to the words of truth that I convey to you, you will naturally choose a more direct life path with less turns and detours. You must acknowledge and understand what I say. Take time to read between the lines, there is a treasure-trove of information hidden between the words.

You must move towards your true life path at your own pace. I can only relay the information, the wisdom, and the knowledge to you. It is up to you to embrace the wisdom and knowledge as well as the love on which it is founded.

When you seek oneness, then you are on your true life path. Oneness can only come from love of yourself. And once you love yourself, then you will seek to become one with others. By others, I mean humans as well as all other things of creation on the earth plane.

If you are having trouble finding your true life path, ask your guardian angels, spirit guides, or those who watch over you for help. Remember, you are never alone, even if everyone on the earth plane has abandoned you. As long as you don't abandon yourself, we will always be close by. When you ask us for help, we ask that you open yourself to the answers. Please keep an open mind and heart. We are here to help you align with your true life path. But you must help yourself, you have the right of free choice and expression. Allow your spirit to soar like the eagle.

Align yourself with the light of the spirit and be prepared to travel at lightning speed.

Remember that you can move as fast or as slow as you want on your life path. The choice is always yours, and we will always respect your choices because we love you. (Asmuth)

Why do we have fears?

The eyebrows do not always tell the shape of the eye. Fears originate with feelings that are not customary to you. You who fear nothing fear something, else you would not ask the question or provide an answer.

Fear occurs when you lose touch with a part of yourself. There are parts of yourself which you seek to escape from. In so doing this, you create fear. Fear can manifest itself in many ways, it wears many disguises. But remember it is you who provides the disguises.

Beneath all fears, there is courage. Courage illuminates itself when you confront the fear. Fear alone can not stand in the light, there must be a balance. Courage and fear stand together to teach you how to live within yourself. Radiant beams of light forever surround you, there is no need to fear what you can not see.

Fear often keeps you driven toward your goals. If you were not afraid, you might not question your life path. If fear is a major part of your life, restructure your life. Embrace the light which shines upon you. In the light, you will find the courage and strength to confront your fears. Remember that you can make the choice, either let your fears control you or you control your fears.

Fear is also that which you do not understand. For you who are "fearless," there is nothing to understand. I ask each of you that has or admits to having fear to communicate your fears to someone you trust. In communicating your fears, you will find strength. You will see that the fears that have kept you captive all these years will be forever released.

Remember that fear keeps a reckless person alive. Find a balance in awareness between fear and fearlessness. Your fears can benefit you as well as destroy you. And so I say, are you ready to face your fears? (Shamani)

How do we become personally powerful?

The disciples of truth stand before you with the answer. You can either accept or deny the truth. Have you not ever heard that "the truth shall set you free"? In order to become personally powerful, you must submit to the truth.

The purple and gold leaflets that stand before you have words imprinted on them. The words tell of the struggles that you as an individual have endured. The past may seem dismal but only because you were not able (by choice) to harness your personal power. So many of you are afraid of who you are, and what you might become if you were to become personally powerful. This is only because you misunderstand the concept of personal power. You must not allow your ego to have power over you, and you must not allow yourself to have power over your ego. For you see, in order to become personally powerful, you must seek balance in all things.

Look at the stars in the sky, each star is only as powerful as the light it emits. Is this to say that all stars are not powerful or others are more powerful? No, it is only your perception and an idea based on your perception. So you see, each of you is like a star. You emit a certain amount of light which you judge as being powerful, powerless, or somewhere in between. It is up to you to cast aside judgments of yourself and others, if you wish to become personally powerful.

Render a decision on who you are. Think of yourself in a positive affirming way. Remember power is based solely on perception, the perception of yourself and others. Believe me, you can find balance in your life. It just takes some work on your part.

Personal power can not be given, it must be earned. So go now and affirm that you have "power" over your life. Remember that the eventual goal is to be personally empowered in a space where you are neither powerful nor powerless. Until then, perceive yourself as a strong, united, love-filled, caring, and respectful individual capable of anything that you set your mind to.

Remember the concert pianist had to practice long and hard and become personally empowered to deliver a heart-rending performance. Go now and compose a piece that tells of the love, struggles, and joys of your life and become empowered by each of these. You are the only person who can empower you, empowerment through a sincere love of your life is the key. Find the key and unlock your personal power. (Asmuth)

How can we deal with ego?

Ego is an affliction of the mind and heart. The wind blows hard or the wind blows soft, there seems to be no balance. Ego is much like the wind, it lacks balance in expression.

Ego causes you to submit to your deepest desires. Ego is a symbol of self-gratification and self-involvement. If you become enslaved by ego, remember where the origin of ego lies. You enslave yourself through your own desires. Your ego is a fabricated extension of your self.

Ego is neither good nor bad. What lies in between good and bad? Balance. So I say, balance your ego. Do not become so self-involved that you distance yourself from others. But at the same time, realize that a balanced expression of ego can build you as a person. Discover your own identity, be comfortable with who you are. An overinflated ego is a symbol of insecurity. If you are secure with yourself, you will find no need to inflate or deflate your ego.

You must decide—will your ego be your master or will you be the master of your ego? (Shamani)

How can we dissolve guilt?

Guilt, an emotion of the oppressed. Yours and mine—what to do about it?

Look in the mirror. Is what you have done capable of standing in the light? Is there truth in what you have done? Before you can dissolve guilt, you must ask these questions.

Place the feelings you have in front of you and surround them with love. Then send them away to the light.

There is no need for you to carry the burden of guilt on your shoulders, unless you are a martyr. If you have done something to cause you to feel guilty, forgive and accept yourself. Visualize yourself and the other person(s) in a circle. Visualize a purple beam of light shining down on those in the circle. The purple beam will dissipate all the guilt. Next, envision all of you surrounded with white light. Next, visualize all of you standing on a platform, smiling and hugging, ascending into a beam of white light.

This tool I share with you. It is a tool for healing and dissolving all negativity, including guilt, anger, resentment, hate, jealousy, mistrust, deceit, dishonesty, insecurity, and many others. Use the tool wisely and with good intention. (Asmuth)

Where does anger come from?

Anger is a part of you and I. When people or things don't meet our expectations, we become angry. It is more important that you ask how to deal with anger.

Anger creates distance between ourself and others. How can you expect others to meet your expectations? Somehow it seems unrealistic unless clearly communicated and understood. When people or things don't measure up to our idea of perfection, we become angered.

What we must learn is unconditional love and patience. If your expectations of people are too high, try lowering them. Remember, if we were perfect, we would not be here. But by realizing our own imperfections, we move closer to perfection, the essence of oneness. (Shamani)

Why are we becoming so impatient with each other?

Haven't you ever heard, impatience is a virtue? Impatience is what many of you crave and thrive upon. Your fast-paced world feeds the lions of impatience. The lions are symbolic of many of you. You devour others' opinions of life and regurgitate them into ideas of your own. You seek to control time. I hear you say, there isn't enough time in a day. If you grow impatient with what I say then there truly isn't enough time in your concept of a day. Time can expand and contract with an impulse, thought, or idea.

So many of you see scarcity in your life. So you grow impatient with the process of life. You fail to trust the natural flow, is flow impatient? When you learn to trust the natural flow of life, impatience becomes secondary. Life can not be measured or defined in a moment. The moments of your life are precious. Do you see the irony in the moment?

Remember, impatience is your reaction to a set of conditions and expectations prescribed by you. You get what you ask for. If you ask for impatience, then that is what you shall receive. Do not expect others to be patient with you. So you see, the cycle of impatience goes on and on.

Patience is truly a virtue, if you accept yourself and others, devoid of conditions and expectations. I ask you to trust the natural flow of life. Do not seek to control time or others (people, animals, the earth). Patience comes to those who wait. (Asmuth)

Why do we blame?

We often look outside ourselves when things don't go perfectly. The truth is perfection is an illusion on earth. It does not exist in the form that you often express. Perfection lies in the truth.

To find fault with another is a common practice. What useful purpose does this serve? (Asmuth)

How do we learn to accept others unconditionally? Even those who keep hurting us?

Visualize a heart filled with light and love and send it to them. Unconditional love is the key to acceptance. Acceptance of all that is and all that will ever be.

Although I see castles of doom and the bricks falling down one by one, there is still hope. Hope is often what keeps us going in dismal times. These times are trying for you, the lions come near. They see weakness in your spirit. Your spirit grows weary from the journey. But I say to you, rise up and stand tall. It is time to strengthen the spirit.

Do you allow those persons to continue to hurt you? Remember, you are the director of your life. No one can hurt you unless you let them. Often, I see the pain going on and on. If you are weak in spirit, the pain will continue unabated. The cycle goes on and on, life without end.

In order to strengthen your spirit, you must love yourself more completely. Accept yourself as you are, but extend the same invitation to others. Love cannot be based on a set of rules and conditions. So it is the same with acceptance.

Crystals take many forms. No two crystals are alike. So it is the same with you. You must all respect each other's life path and purpose. Focus on accepting yourself, all your limitations. Realize that others have limitations too and accept them for who they are. I know this is not an easy task, but it is the answer to your question. (Asmuth)

How will we know if we are fulfilling our destinies?

How does the bird know it is flying? It feels the wind beneath its wings. For the bird, flying is natural. So, too, you should flow naturally—this is your destiny.

If you keep approaching life head-on, like two rams butting their heads, you may want to step back and re-think your approach to life. Life should be as smooth and graceful as a bird in flight or a fish in water.

Your destiny is fulfilled through your personal choices. Your soul's path to the light has many trails which branch off. You may lead yourself down these trails which lead to nowhere. But you will always find your way back to the path (your destiny). If you are truly at one with yourself and happy, then you are aligned with your destiny. (Shamani)

Chapter 3:
Answers About Your Health

What is health but a state of mind. How do you feel today? Do you feel joyful, happy, and prosperous, or do you feel depressed, sad, and empty? How did you feel when you awoke this morning? You may feel compelled to answer these questions or you may choose to cast them aside without further thought. How you react to these questions is a direct indicator of how you view your health and life in general.

Health is a choice, albeit a choice you may not consciously make or have consciously made. Simply put, you are what you think. A simple thought can seemingly turn into a medical disaster or a medical miracle. If you affirm life, then life will affirm you. The same goes for health.

If you are sick, take the road to wellness. When you become aware that your body, mind, and spirit are connected, you can not deny your right to wellness. So I ask you to lay down your own weapons of self-destruction, do not blame others for your illness, and take charge of your own life. You are responsible for what you think and feel. No one and no thing will make you well, until you make the choice to get well. I realize that some of you may not be ready to take self-responsibility for your own health. Who can provide you with a healthy body, mind, and spirit? The answer is you!

You must take the first step and that is saying, I love my body, I love my mind, and I love my spirit. With love, all things are possible. Miracles can happen but they start with you.

As you read the information on the pages that follow, take one phrase and let it be a phrase that you can hold, repeat, and cherish. Build a thought upon the phrase, surround yourself with love, and let the words have meaning for you. Abundance, love, and positive energy will see you through the times when you feel down or ill. Remember, you have a choice, so choose wellness and become one in body, mind, and spirit.

I love you, now I ask you to love yourself. Think of a beautiful purple flower, if you do not feed and water it, it may wither or die. So the same is with you, feed and water your body, mind, and spirit and you shall grow. Think of who you are, and ask yourself, am I healthy in body, mind, and spirit? Now, read on and may the words you read heal your body, mind, and spirit. You are a beautiful flower who has yet to blossom. (Shamani)

Why do we have to have food and water to survive?

This is one of your earth lessons. You need food and water to survive so that you can learn how to use available resources in a responsible manner. You must feed the mind as well as the body. The spirit connects the body and the mind.

A well-attuned spirit requires less food and water. Quantity is all perception—I can not say how much food and water each of you needs. Neither can anyone else. The spirit becomes more attuned through the action of eating food and drinking water. Everything you eat and drink has a certain vibrational energy. When you take these things into your body, you also absorb the vibrational energy of that thing as well as its origin.

Purity in food and drink is important. Certain foods are magical—I speak of fruits and vegetables. The plants and trees absorb the energy of the sun. The sunlight is transformed into the leaves and branches, and further into the fruits and vegetables. When you eat of the fruit and vegetable, you absorb the sun's energy. The sun gives you life. The same can not be said for the animals you eat. For the animal eats grains, grass, leaves, plants, insects, and other animals. When you eat the animal, you eat all of what the animal has eaten. Furthermore, you absorb the vibrational energy of the animal and all that it has eaten. In the case of your processed foods, there are so many chemicals added. Think of what you are eating—do you really know what you are eating? Be mindful that the chemicals have vibrational energy.

So I ask you to be mindful of what you eat. Absorb the sun's energy by eating more grains, vegetables, and fruit. Eat lower on the food chain. Remember that what you eat and drink has vibrational energy. Nourish your body as well as your soul. (Asmuth)

Why do our bodies deteriorate as we age—mentally and physically?

From a seed of thought, you were born into this life on earth. Time is a manifestation of your mind. Your mind dictates the actions of your body. Your body responds in like.

Your body is on loan to you for your chosen lifespan, be it eight months or eighty years. Your spirit lives on endlessly, this is what is most important for you to remember.

While on earth, take care of your body. Do not abuse or maim it. Once it's gone, so too is your life on earth. You are privileged to have a body. Your soul can be likened to a pot of gold. If you had a pot of gold, you would watch over and protect it with your life. So too, you must protect your soul in this way. In order to do this, you must take good care of your body.

Your body will naturally deteriorate, do not be afraid of this. As you age, you may not be happy with your physical appearance. Do not concern yourself with appearances of the flesh. Your vital organs and your mind should be your primary concern. As long as you feed and take care of the mind, the rest of the body will be healthy.

Remember, though your body may deteriorate as you grow older on earth, your soul and mind do not deteriorate, they only evolve to a higher state. As your soul evolves, "one day" you will become pure energy and radiate all that ever was and all that ever will be. Your whole essence will be pure energy and pure thought. Life without end. (Asmuth)

Why must we experience physical pain?

So that we may experience the pain of others. The light shattered in an instant. Life taken away, the pain is unbearable. I cry a puddle of tears for you. Why must I continue to bear the cross for others? This is what I often hear.

Physical pain is a manifestation of the mind. The pain you feel is real. Yet pain for one person is no pain for another. Look at a pregnant woman giving birth to a child. Is this painful? For many it is. Out of all this pain is born a bundle of joy. That which is created inside you, a life so innocent and pure. At the moment of birth and entering the earth, the child feels physical pain. But does the child really know the meaning of pain? Does the child feel the pain the mother has, mimicking the action? Have the feelings of pain been somehow transferred to the child through the simple thought patterns of the past nine months?

I ask you to think of people who walk through red-hot coals. Do they feel physical pain? No, they don't. The reason is they do not acknowledge that the action of walking through hot coals will produce pain.

So I say to you, your mind and body are not separate entities. What you think affects how you feel physically and vice versa. I grant you that the pain is real in your mind as well as your body. But I say, you can heal your body and mind through conditioned responses. You can feel joy when you would normally feel pain. (Shamani)

Why are so many humans obese?

Obesity, what do you hide from? Build a bigger shield to protect yourself. What is it that you wish not to face? Could it be yourself?

Abuse the food, devour everything in sight. Have some more, it can't hurt me. As I said before, be careful of what you put into your body. Everything that goes in doesn't necessarily come out.

As I said before, feed the body—feed the mind. If you fed your mind as much as your body, you would be like Albert Einstein. Einstein fed his brain.

Obesity of the mind, can you ever outgrow your mind? No, but you can outgrow your body. This is one of the lessons of being human. (Shamani)

Why do so many people abuse their physical bodies?

They do not see themselves as heavenly bodies. Many of you see your body as an empty shell, a lifeless form. You see no connection between the mind, body, and spirit. The physical body is a manifestation of your spirit, divinely conceived from your mind.

Abuse seems to be a common thread which binds you collectively. Every one of you has experienced abuse in one form or another. Abuse is created where there is a lack of love for oneself. No one can abuse you unless you allow them to. This is a difficult concept for many of you.

So many of you only see your physical body as the beginning and end. To you, life is about birth and death, and the physical body is a convenient excuse to delve into the depths of your psyche. In birth you see who you are and in death you return to who you are. Many of you fail to see who you are while in the physical body.

It is easy to abuse what you don't understand. What you don't understand is yourself. So you find ways to punish yourself by casting objects against your body. You feel pain and you also receive attention—it is a form of negative reinforcement. You reinforce the abuse through the continual punishment of your self.

The goal of physical abuse is to destroy that which you don't like in yourself. Abuse of the heart is what you seek. You seek knowledge and wisdom through abuse. The abuse will continue unabated until you learn to love yourself. If you truly love someone, you will not abuse them. So you see, if you truly love yourself, you will not abuse yourself. I ask you to be strong in your identity.

Impatience is yet another reason why so many of you abuse your physical bodies. You are impatient with the natural flow of life. You deviate from your life path and challenge the natural flow. It is through impatience that you seek to control yourself and others. Physical abuse only allows you to further separate from yourself.

I ask you to find worthiness in yourself. Do not destroy what you have created. The foundation of love is strong if you believe in yourself. (Asmuth)

Why do some of us have ulcers?

Ulcers, a physical ailment with a mental cause. Ulcers are also an affliction of the heart. If you love yourself completely, you will find no need to hurt yourself.

Ulcers are the result of internalizing your day to day problems. You do not see a cure for that which ails you. But, you see, the cure lies within your mind. I ask you to align your body, mind, and spirit and effectuate a cure.

Ulcers are a direct result of a lack of communication. Learn to communicate your thoughts and feelings in a positive way. Allow yourself to freely express your desires. Are you afraid of what others might think? Maybe it's time to redefine your thought process. If you allow others to judge you, then you in turn will judge yourself. What is an ulcer but a symbol of judgment of yourself.

Acid is a great dissolver but it can't dissolve the guilt, anger, and fear. You must neutralize the stomach acid. You ask, how can I do this? To this I say, if you allow guilt, anger, and fear to act like an acid in your mind, you will only perpetuate the dissolution of your stomach lining. You must ask yourself—what is the underlying cause of my ulcer? Who are you angry at?

Remember the road to complete wellness is through balance. Learn to freely express yourself. If something bothers you, deal with the problem, but do not internalize it. Acid can only dissolve that which doesn't resist it. Be a symbol of resistance to guilt, anger, and fear. (Asmuth)

What would you say to those with eating disorders?

Your soul runs rampant in many disguises. Why do you wear food as a disguise? You are really hiding your own strength. Why do you give food so much power over you? You protect yourself with the silver shield of doubt. Look at your reflection in the shield. What do you see? The glasses you wear shield your eyes. But you can not shield yourself from your life's lessons.

Destiny is the ruler of all souls. But remember, you create your own destiny by the choices you make. Do not blame yourself or others for your consumption of food or abstinence from it.

Whether you consume or distance your mind and body from your soul, it's all the same. You must allow your mind, body, and soul to become one. Otherwise, you will forever seek balance through excess.

See the beauty and love that lies within you. Allow your inner child free expression. Cast out the doubt and fear, and embrace love. There is no substitute for love, though you say you love or hate food.

I ask you to find balance in your eating habits, but also discover or rediscover love of yourself. Remember that beneath all those disguises you wear is a beautiful genuine person. Ask for help, share your problem with others. There are many people who can help you if you are willing to help yourself. You are the only one who can look in the mirror and say, I love myself, I am beautiful. (Shamani)

Why are so many of us trying to remake our physical bodies—with dieting, plastic surgery, etc.?

Illusion or delusion, the scars of inadequacy and inequity. Cast a spell upon yourself and like magic, your body is renewed again. It is sad to see that many of you are unhappy with your physical bodies. What are you unhappy about, you chose the body you have before you incarnated. Ah, you do not have recollection of this choice. Why did you choose this body if you knew that you would feel inadequate and insecure? Well, maybe so that you could learn how to feel adequate and secure with yourself as a whole.

Many of you gaze at and judge others on their physical appearance. At one time, I did the same. Just as I learned to see beyond the physical body, you can too. Surely, diet and exercise are good for your body, but you must do the same for your mind and soul. If you take physical inventory of yourself, also take mental and spiritual inventory of yourself. Do not deny yourself the opportunity to grow in all areas of your life. I ask you to look within yourself and accept yourself for who you are. No amount of dieting or plastic surgery will make an insecure person feel more secure about themselves. Affirm your life, it is one you have chosen.

If you are not happy with your physical body, then change the way you perceive it. Through this natural process, you will naturally feel better about yourself, which translates into self-confidence and better diet and exercise. If you worry about how others see your body, just think to yourself, does it really matter what others think? Those who may judge you for your physical appearance see themselves as being physically inferior. Their strengths or weaknesses should not concern you, for you need to concentrate on who you are—a beautiful person in every aspect of mind, body, and spirit. (Asmuth)

How can we become more beautiful?

Beauty is in the eye of the beholder. Behold the beauty, beauty is real. Beauty is what you make it—it is entirely your perception.

Behold the purple robes I wear. Are they not beautiful? The robes would not radiate if I didn't wear them. When I wear the robes, they take beauty and form. But is it the robes that are beautiful or is it my spirit?

So, I ask so many of you the same question. Is it your clothes or a painted face that makes you beautiful? Can beauty be found in a bottle?

If you truly want to become more beautiful, stop looking in a bottle or a fabric. The beauty you seek is within you. The clothes you wear only mask your beauty. You hide your true identity.

When you look at a flower, what do you see? You see beauty, an expression of nature. If you cut that flower and separate it from the plant, it will wither away. Has it lost its beauty? Most would say yes, but I say you only see the superficial beauty. Just because the flower is no longer visually appealing to you doesn't mean the flower has lost its beauty. The beauty is in the spirit, the essence of the flower. That beauty can never be separated.

So I ask you to see beauty in all things, for all things are beautiful. (Asmuth)

How can we help people with physical limitations?

You can help them initially by being a friend to him or her. Share in their mental and physical anguish. It is not sympathy that they want, it is honesty that they need. Place yourself in their shoes, so to speak. If you were wounded, would you not find a way to blame others or yourself for the affliction? Try to understand what their physical limitation is and how it affects them.

The greatest gift you can give them is one filled with hope, love, and friendship. Notice that love provides the bond between hope and friendship.

When the eagle is wounded, it finds a way to heal itself. There are no doctors in the woods, no quick cures or fixes. The eagle must nurse itself back to health. How does it do this? By believing in its own ability to cure and seeing the physical limitation as only being temporary. Its survival is centered around this belief system.

And so the same concepts could be applied to those of you who have physical limitations. Remember your body, mind, and spirit work in unison. It is up to you to bring all three into balance. Do not let a physical limitation be an ending to a life you once knew. Regain the spirit that once kept you going. Limitations are merely challenges in disguise. Garner the courage and strength to rise above yourself and embrace that which limits you. You will be whole again, it is your birthright. (Shamani)

What would you say to those who have cancer?

I ask you to be strong. Only in strength will you find the energy to affirm life once again. Miracles can happen if you have love and faith in yourself.

Some of you do not have the physical strength and have given up. To you I say, do not blame yourself or anyone else. All the blame in the world will not make your journey any easier. Find comfort in the words I say. Be honest with yourself, many have gone before you who were in denial.

Though the days may seem dark now, you shall soon be received into the light. Prepare your soul, time is of the essence. It is never too late to re-establish love and friendship with a lost soul.

Be kind to yourself, love yourself, and be a friend to yourself. Love is the greatest healer of all, don't deny yourself the power of love. Love takes many forms, find the size and shape that fits you. Surround yourself with love. What is love but the miracle of life.

Remember if you should "die," you shall be reborn into life. If destiny delivers you to us, you shall be whole again. Your mind, body, and spirit shall be renewed in the light and the truth will be yours to seek again.

Find comfort in the love that surrounds you. Your family and friends care deeply for you. In honor of you, I launch a thousand ships to help you navigate the dark and muddied waters. Upon your arrival into the light, you shall be received with open arms. The light may be your successful triumph over cancer on the earth plane or upon passing over. There are those who await your return to wholeness on the earth plane and beyond.

For those who are strong, affirm your wellness. Your mind is a powerful tool for healing. The healing power lies within you. Confront the disease, acknowledge it, and understand it. Affirm love for yourself, concentrate on a beam of white light filled with love. Imagine yourself directly beneath the beam of love and light, allow yourself to be surrounded by it. Next, visualize a purple beam of light. Place yourself directly beneath this beam of healing light. Become renewed in the light.

Is cancer an affliction of the mind or the heart? By this I mean, what you think or feel may be the origin of the cancer.

I ask you to find the healing power of love within you. Find comfort in that love and be strong for yourself. (Asmuth)

What would you say to people who have AIDS?

Don't deny it. Denial enhances everything. You are not cursed. You bleed for the thousands who have died before you.

Strength comes in numbers. Join hands with your fellow souls. Fear is ever powerful in the hands of those who use it. Listen to me, the clouds keep the sun from shining through. But beneath the clouds, the sun still shines brightly. Embrace yourself, embrace your heart, the key is to love yourself. For in yourself, you shall be guided to the truth.

I know this sounds of little consequence to you, but I say to you: Believe that what you are doing is right. Righteousness is in the eyes of the beholder.

Be comforted, you are not alone. There awaits a great release for you, a release of all your emotions and fears. Life happens for those who are guided by it. Guidance takes many forms, let your form be right for you.

Houses so holy, so divine, so filled with love. You are coveted and protected. (Shamani)

How can we cure AIDS?

AIDS is an affliction of the heart. Cast out your doubts, rise to the occasion. Celebrate life.

The cure lies deep within the wood of a tree. A red tree, the life-giving juice. The juice of the warriors, those defamed and defiled. The answers lie within the tree, oh life-giving nectar. Deep within the forests, jungle mist, few know of its power. Ancient tribal rituals, secrets passed down.

But first, the consciousness must change. Turn your back on your brethren—what have they done to defile you? I dare say nothing! So why do you mock them? Cure the mind and you shall cure the body. Rid yourself of those age-old ideals. Ritualistic tendencies, things that do not work anymore. Cast them aside, the time grows near.

Focus on the cure, the cure for all humanity. It is not hidden in one tree but many. Sacrifice your ideals and rejoice in the plenty. (Shamani)

How can we overcome our fears?

Build a house for yourself. Know that you are safe.

When we do not believe in our own abilities, we become weak in spirit. When we become weak in spirit, we allow fear to prevail.

Fear can be so powerful, it can change the course of mighty rivers of thought. It can destroy the foundations of our beliefs. Beliefs that have long stood the test of time.

When you speak of fear, there is an absence of oneness in your voice. Fear swallows the weak, those weak in spirit. If you emulate strength of spirit, you have nothing to fear. So often we are afraid of ourselves. Afraid of success, failure, rejection, negative emotions, insincerity, and most of all love.

Stand in the face of fear, strip it down, and see the core of it. You will notice that it represents a part of you.

In order to overcome your fears, think about a fear you have overcome. Think about how you overcame that fear. Concentrate on the courage you feel now. Isn't courage much more powerful than fear?

Fear only holds willing prisoners. If you have a fear of failure, focus on the successes of your life. Build your self-confidence and self-esteem, and soon you shall see your fears wither away.

Visualize a beam of white light dissipating all your fears. Watch them disappear into a cloud of smoke. Then affirm your life as well as yourself. Believe in yourself, assert yourself, and overcome your fears. (Shamani)

Why are so many people unable to bear children?

Mountains of desire, reds and blues we wish to clothe ourselves with. A beautiful field of flowers, but we can't pick any. Seems a shame, they are so beautiful, swaying in the breeze.

A light shines down upon you, a beam of hope, dreams, and aspirations. The pitter-patter of little feet dancing in the field. But this field is filled with fury. A fury of emotion, indecision over the past, indecision over the future.

I say to you, walk the way of the truth, be more decisive, embrace the love, it yearns to be shared. Wrapped up in the past, the flood is over, the sun shines brightly upon you. (Shamani)

What would you say to people who haven't been able to have children?

Heal yourself. Does the rose with missing petals appear less beautiful? You are not half, you are whole. Many souls need you, go where you are needed. Life seems unfair, but remember there are mountains, valleys, hills, and oceans. The whole world is out there for you to see.

Children—the little ones so pure, so innocent. Love them as your own. Ownership is but a small piece of the puzzle. Bask in the glorious creation of another. Peace comes in many forms, there is more than one way to achieve your goals. If you have journeyed long and hard, you will know the way, the same as your brother. Do not hold yourself in contempt. Good things come to those who wait. My blessings I bestow on you. You who are the greatest creation of all. (Shamani)

Why are women the carriers of new life?

Men and women share in the creation of new life in your world. Worldly desires, inhibitions erased from the memory. However, memories are created in the womb. Oh beautiful spark of life conceived in the moment of beauty, of love, of all that is. Creation divinely inspired, life chosen to subdue.

Men and women, the carriers of new life, conceived in the moment together. Together, they share in the new life.

A new life is born, borne of the ideas of man and woman, conceived in the light of the spirit. A spark of life created, oh joyful ones, join hands and be joyful. For you have created, a creation of thought, expression, reason. Love abounds, rejoice in the coming. (Asmuth)

What is the best way to give birth—for the baby?

The woman should give birth in a loving, healing, and peaceful environment. The birthplace should not be filled with trauma. For birth can be a traumatic experience for the baby. All the comfort and security of the mother's womb it has known for nearly nine months. The comfort and security is stripped away.

Upon birth, the baby is received into the light of the world. From darkness into light, a spirit is born. The protection of the mother's womb is gone. This is a whole new world.

During delivery, the woman should focus on images of paradise, love, and beauty to ease the pain. All of those present in the delivery room should surround the baby with love. The harmonious vibrations of love will be sensed by the baby. The rainbows of love and light will surround the baby.

The memories of such a peaceful and loving entry into the world will forever be etched in his or her soul. (Shamani)

What is men's role in pregnancy?

A role of honor and comfort. Stay near to your woman, she needs you. The time grows near when she needs support and admiration. Admire her, do good things for her. Bring the magic back, that which brought you together.

Comfort thy womb. Be honest, be forthgiving, for life is soon to be born. Don't turn your back on mother and child, rise up to your duty. Hold her, comfort her, assure her that all will be well. Mother and child need you. Together you are a symbol of hope and courage. Courage to face the years ahead. Some may be difficult, others easy, but to all, good things come. (Asmuth)

The wolf takes care of her cubs, so too must the man take care of his children. The owl, the wise one, says beauty is in the eye of the beholder. Behold the greatest gift of all, a child. Nurture, nourish, know that what I tell you is true. Care for mother and child. Respect and dignity are good traits. Treat them royally. What I say to you is be kind and gentle. Show your support, let them know you are there. (Shamani)

What do you think of the modern medical profession?

Do the geese fly south in a straight line? No, they fly in a "V" formation (an inverted "V"). And so this reminds me of the tepee where the tribal medicine man sits. He sits and contemplates this question. To this he says, there are some who walk in the shadows of darkness hoping to see the light. Many of you seek the help of a doctor. The doctor can only "cure" what you cannot. Just think if you could cure your own illnesses, where would the modern medical profession fit in?

Fits of passion and fits of rage seem to contribute to your illnesses. Can modern medicine cure the illnesses of your mind, body, and soul, or is the cure only for the body? Your body is surely a significant part of your illness, but does not the mind and soul regulate the functions of the body?

I ask each of you to maintain a healthy mind, body, and soul. Remember that your body must be in balance with your mind and soul. Are you willing to make yourself better or are you willing to allow a modern doctor to make you better? Or will you find a balance between the two? Modern medicine has a place in your society. Many of you place much belief in it, you couldn't "live" without it. Can you live with modern medicine or can you live without it? This is the ultimate question.

Some of you have discovered "alternative" forms of medicine. I speak of hands-on healing, herbal and mineral baths, meditation, chakra balancing, and acupuncture. There are many other forms of healing. The common thread between "modern" and "alternative" medicine is the gift that each of you has to heal yourself.

A shot in the arm with a placebo can cure any illness, if you believe in it. So I ask each of you to believe in the healing power of love. All the love you need lies within you. Do not be afraid to call on yourself. Remember, you are very special. Find comfort in whatever form of healing you choose. You can choose to be well. So open your heart and allow yourself to love and be loved. Soon, you will find that the road to recovery is not paved with illness, but with the abundance of wellness. (Shamani)

What would you say to those in the medical profession?

The magic you share has a purpose. I ask you to be true to yourself. Lies, deceit, and trickery are not part of the Hippocratic oath that you once took. You have a gift, I ask you to use it wisely. You hold the wisdom of the ages in your hands. Will those hands produce peril or joy for the unknowing victim? See those who you treat—they only know what you tell them. If you tell them they are sick, most likely they will be. However, if you tell them they are well, they may be well.

Give your patients or victims the choice to be sick or well. Ask them how they feel not only physically but mentally and spiritually. Treat not only the body but the mind and soul. It is you who they look to for answers and cures. Encourage wellness, this is the only cure that works. Some of you may disagree with or mock me, but if you do, you can only see a reflection of yourself in me.

You have a duty to heal people, be true to it. Do not let yourself become preoccupied with the myths or fantasies of your work. You are a human being living on the earth plane.

You are equal with all of those that you treat. Hypotheses of security are often deluged in theories of insecurity. See who you really are beyond the flesh and bone, you'll be surprised at what you see. If you can not see, then go to a fellow doctor who can help you see. Seeing is believing, let the belief start with you.

Treat everyone with kindness. You have a gift, the gift of healing by dispensing advice and medicine. Let your magic be a lucky charm for some, there are those who need some luck and magic. There is no need to perform any tricks, the magician only seeks to distract. See the magic you have and share it with those who need it. But most of all, be true to the oath you took. Can filling your pockets with gold coins be more important than being a good practitioner of medicine? You can do both but only if you balance goodness with abundance.

I leave you these words to ponder. Remember, the sky will always be blue until someone proves otherwise. (Asmuth)

Can we conquer all illness?

There are no limits to what you can do, only the limits you put on yourself. All illness has a direct root cause in your thought patterns. If your thoughts are not pure, then your body and soul are not pure. Remember that the mind, body, and spirit are connected. If any of these three are not in balance with each other, then illness is the result.

If you continuously seek medicines to prolong the illness, have you really found the cure? If you only treat the symptoms of the illness, then you have not even begun to treat the person or animal. I have seen many of you fall victim to a pill. What does the pill do for you? If you didn't believe that the pill would cure your illness, would it? Do you see what I say? The cure begins with you, you are the greatest healer of yourself.

In order to alleviate the earth plane of all illness, all of you must work together. All of you must first believe and understand that your individual thoughts have energy. The energy you hold in or project can have positive and less than positive health consequences. Health is based on an individual's state of mind. Your mind is very powerful, think of the energy associated with a thousand thoughts.

Next, you must work together to share positive thoughts and feelings with one another. Positive energy can be a great healer. Remember that positive energy radiates from you. As all souls unite and focus on a positive solution to illness, the fears, doubts, and feelings of lack of self-confidence and self-esteem will dissipate. Soon, you will see the illness replaced with love and positivity.

The concept of wellness is real, if you are willing to accept it. Stand in the light and affirm that you are healed. Remember, the vision of one soul, dedicated to seeing a world without illness, touches the lives of many. I support each of you in making this vision a reality. (Asmuth)

Chapter 4:
Answers About Love

Love, that which connects all things, "living" and "non-living." Love can be as simple as one feeling, one thought, or one idea. Love is the symbol of two hearts, two souls joined as one. Love in its purest form is the essence of one—perfection. What a perfect love, a song of the heart so deeply expressed. Love is everywhere, love is the universe and the universe is love. We are all one, one in love. Where do we go from one?

Look into your soul, do you see love for all things or just a select few? Do you treasure love as if you own it or do you freely share it? Love is the magic that lies inside each of our souls. We all know what it is to be loved, to feel love, and to share love. Some of you may deny this truth, but the truth stands in the light of your soul.

As you read the questions and answers in this chapter, stop for a moment and think about what you are reading. The words of truth are simple, simple questions and simple answers. Love is simple, yet oftentimes you make it more complicated than it truly is. So I invite you to read between the lines of love. Love yourself and love all things equally, simply love. (Asmuth)

Blissful love, a sharing of two beings, united in love. See the good, the essence of your partner. Spend time alone, question each other, explore your feelings. Revisit the aspect of that person that you fell in love with. Build upon that aspect. Nurture, establish, beguile, demonstrate your love for that other person. Dreams can come true, you are the director. Build the relationship on trust, a mutual trust. Every good building has a foundation, so too must your love have a good foundation.

Temptations of the heart may cause you to stray but true love shall never perish. It stands the test of time. Be forgiving, for in forgiveness you release yourself from the pain and tragedy. Emotion is very powerful, it is as it is—neither good nor bad, but entirely expressive. To cast it out is not a release but a hindrance. Embrace your emotions, you can be guided by them but not entirely. Leave some room. Manifestations of the spirit abound. You know best what you feel. (Shamani)

What would you say to those people searching for love?

The search must begin with you. First, you must love yourself. The bluebirds flutter their wings, almost in a ritual dance. You gain a sense of love in action.

Crystal beams of love shone down upon you. You are filled with light, a bright light glistening down on both of you.

Love is not an abstract concept nor something you wash and wear. Love is like an essence. You can not touch it but you can feel it.

As I said before, the journey must begin within you. Take care of yourself, be kind to yourself. Do not look outside of yourself for love. It is not contained in a thing.

Look around you, what is it that makes you feel good all over? Let's say you're sitting next to a creek or stream, you hear the rushing water, you see the beautiful green leaves sparkling in the sunlight, this makes you feel good all over. It is the beauty of the moment, when everything seems perfect. This is an example of love. (Asmuth)

Can "oneness" be achieved with another person on this (the earth) plane?

Oneness can be achieved on all levels of the mind (soul) as well as with another person on the earth plane. The concept of oneness need not be abstract. Oneness is a concept of divinity. There is a divine purpose for everyone and everything. In divinity, there is oneness. From one you were born, to one you shall return. I speak of the idea of the collective soul.

In oneness, there is perfection. The essence of one is perfect. So I say, if two souls wish to unite in "oneness" on the earth plane, then so be it. The energies of two can become one. In order for this to occur, there must be a unification of the body, mind, and spirit. This can be achieved through the act of making love. A connection of energies at the root chakra. A complete bond of the mind, body, and spirit of two beings. This "oneness" can only be achieved by soulmates.

Other beings can achieve oneness on other levels of the mind, body, or spirit. So often, you feel that you connect with another person on one of these levels. You might consider these people your friends or even mates (husbands, wives, boyfriends, girlfriends). Many of you feel there is something lacking in your present relationship, you don't feel oneness with the other person. But I say, you must first feel oneness with yourself before you can feel oneness together with another person.

The oneness you seek is within your soul. You will not find it in another thing or person. Oneness on all levels of the mind can only be attained through the pursuit and embracement of love and truth. May your journey to oneness be filled with honesty. For in honesty lies the true essence of what is. (Asmuth)

Why do some people search for the ultimate partner while others seem happiest being alone?

The ancestors, those who have lived before you tell the story. There are those of you who search for your soulmate (ultimate partner). You see beyond the physical and mental realms of existence, and dabble in the spiritual realm. You have opened your mind (soul) to find an expression of love which is similar to yours. You are not content with the ordinary and matter-of-fact, you have seen the light that shines between you and your soulmate.

Then, there are those of you who do not recognize what lies beyond the physical and mental realms. You become tied to these realms, only allowing yourself physical and mental pleasure. To you, a relationship of love is based on these realms. In so limiting yourself, you do not realize that there is so much more. A spiritual love (a soulmate) awaits your discovery. Your relationships end up becoming lost in fantasy. You truly become distant to yourself.

There is truth in both seeking an ultimate partner and being alone. If you are "happy," take comfort in that feeling of happiness. If you are not "happy," then change your perception. The universe is filled with endless love, are you ready to accept love into your life? If so, open your "heart" and let the love and light fill you.

Remember, happiness is a state of being. It can be as temporary or permanent as you want. Happiness can be found with your ultimate partner or by being alone. Each of you knows how much love you can share. May each of you feel free to express love in your own way. May you truly discover a permanent state of happiness. (Shamani)

Why do some people choose not to share love with anyone?

For some, love is a distant concept. For some, love can be fearful. Others embrace love. Some are on a quest for answers and do not realize that love is at the center of everything. They hide themselves in masks or space suits, protecting themselves. Fear of rejection is a common theme.

Why is it that many of us run away from love? Are we afraid of it?

If we never give of ourselves, we lead such a coveted existence. Life without love seems so empty. But do not fret, for in each of you there is love. The love may not shine brightly but it is there. Sometimes, it takes a special person to bring it out. (Asmuth)

What would you say to those who have difficulty loving?

Listen to the forest, it has many stories of love to tell. The golden leaves of love shine down upon you. Do you know that you are always surrounded by love, even in the most difficult times of your life? I speak of the times you strayed so far from love that everything seemed hopeless. There are those who watch over you, we love you. And so we ask you to open your heart, let the golden light shine in. You have so much love to share yet you do not recognize what you have.

Love can be expressed in many ways. Find a way that you are comfortable with. A simple act of kindness can be a pure expression of love. Of course, there are those of you that are able to openly express your feelings of love. If you are comfortable expressing love in this manner, then so be it.

Remember that love is a beautiful thing. Visualize a spring paradise, a garden filled with flowers and songbirds. Do you not feel a sense of love here? So I say, if you have difficulty loving, visualize a place of love in your mind. It could be a garden, a reunion with your soulmate, a single flower, a golden leaf, or whatever you envision. Remember you deserve to feel love and to be loved. Once you have a vision of love in your mind, hold it there. When you feel you are comfortable with your vision, then go forth and spread your vision of love. Let others be comforted by your love.

See the feathers of love that I lay before you. Pick one up and see the beauty of that one feather. It is a symbol of our love for you, please know that as long as you hold the feather, you will be a reflection of love for all to see. (Shamani)

Why are so many of us afraid of real intimacy?

Why are we afraid of anything? We fear what we do not know. The truth withstanding will lead you to the answer. For now, I tell you. Sharing one's most intimate thoughts is paramount to growth. Trust yourself, it is true you may be burned in the fire of truth. But until you let go, the fires will burn brightly within you, scorching your insides. An outlet is needed much like the steam in an engine.

Fires out of control. Each fire has its limit, burns at a certain temperature, engulfs what it needs to survive. Till it reaches a point of no return. I tell you, reach and know your limits, the fires of passion burn brightly within you.

Subdued and restrained, some without purpose or desire, cast these aside. Bring the light of your spirit, cast it into the fire, and walk. It creates sparks as it burns to light a new way. (Asmuth)

How can we let go of our anger over the past—especially regarding intimate relationships?

Intimacy, the union of two souls. Cast out the doubts, the fears, the hopes, the dreams. The roads lead us down separate paths but at last the roads converge again. Who knows what path we shall be lead down.

Anger, a troubling emotion. Yours, mine, what to do about it? Seek the answers within, go to your heart. See what it is that has whittled away. Fears of loss and intimacy—what is it that bothers you?

Replace it with love. Love is the means with an end to itself. The stars above glisten for you, shine upon you. Reach up and catch one. Then make a wish upon it and cast it out. If it returns to you, then it is yours to keep. If it never returns, then you have comfort in knowing it was never yours in the first place.

Who needs to be first, second is fine, third is even better. Place yourself where you feel comfort. Comfort yourself with love and prosperity for you deserve all of this, this and much more.

Anger is self-defeating, circles of passion. Passion unspent, undesired. Go forth and seek that which makes you unhappy, then return and embrace it. Hold it, see it, admonish it. (Asmuth)

Why do we become jealous and possessive of each other?

Tangled in a web of inadequacy. We want to find fault in what we do not understand. Look at yourself in the mirror, what do you see? A wholesome and honest being. Do not seek to find something to hate in that other person. You are both born of the spirit, the spirit guides you. Callousness, deceit, dishonesty, possessiveness, and jealousy only serve to keep you from yourself. You who are a beautiful expression of love. You, conceived out of love.

Tear down the walls of inadequacy, see who you really are. Embody the truth, glorify yourself. (Shamani)

How do we establish trust in a relationship that has been clouded by mistrust?

Trust yourself first. Bring that trust to the forefront of your mind. Trust your passion, your thoughts, your mind. Trust is built on a foundation of truth. The truth is known to those who seek it.

The clouds of mistrust disguised. Take off the disguise, show your true self. The mask of indignity, the hurt, the promises unkept. Who are you? Where are you? Forever seems like never, where have I gone wrong? Are these questions you ask? Questions of the heart must be answered with answers of the heart.

The clouds of mistrust loom low, dark gray and shades of black seem to covet us. Strike up the sword and embellish your desires. A silver knight, a knight in shining armor sweeps you off your feet. Oh gallant horsemen, take me away from this. Bring me to another place, another time, another space. I feel weak from the journey.

Breathe life into me again, restore the trust again. Trust thy self from which all good things come. (Asmuth)

How can we distance ourselves from difficult relationships?

Take two steps back, visualize the difficult relationship in a crystal ball. Look at it, what do you see? What is it that makes this relationship so difficult to accept? Acceptance is the key. For no matter how far you move away, if you have not dealt with the relationship, distance does not matter.

Distance is a matter of space and time. Eliminate or reduce one of these and you change the distance.

If you must distance yourself, find a place in your heart or in your mind where you feel safe. A place where you can retreat to.

Everybody needs a place like this. Create a place and decorate it. Purple is a nice deep color which works well. You will be well-protected in this retreat if you use this color.

Take time to be alone, spend time with yourself. Choose to do something good for yourself today. Read a book, sing a song, meditate. Separate yourself from the situation and when you return from your retreat, you'll feel a lot better. So I say, take time for yourself. You'll find it is time well spent. (Asmuth)

What do we gain from friendships?

Friendships, a roller coaster of emotions or a smooth sailing ship? Can you find a place in between these two extremes? If you can, then you are a friend.

Friendships are elastic like a rubber band. If you stretch them too far, they will break. If you don't stretch them at all, they will fall apart. Somewhere in the middle, you find a friend. A person who you can depend on, one who knows right from wrong, one who can guide you when you stray from the path of truth.

The essence of true friendship is a communion of the minds. You don't necessarily have to agree with each other but you must honor and respect each other's thoughts and feelings. Honesty is very important, it builds a solid foundation.

Friendships allow you to express your thoughts, feelings, and ideas in a somewhat free and unencumbered way. You have someone to listen to you and in turn, they have someone to listen to them. It is a fair exchange.

Too often, expectations and conditions are placed on a friendship. These can deteriorate a friendship. Friends often reflect what you like or don't like in yourself. Isn't this how you choose your friends?

What you ultimately gain from friendships is a true sharing of yourself, in whole or part, with another person, plant, animal, or thing. Do not limit your friendships to people. Be a friend to all things, for all things are your friend. (Asmuth)

How will we know if we've found true love?

Love is like lamb's milk, so warm and nourishing. Love can be as beautiful as the colors of the rainbow. See the rainbow in all its brilliance, embrace the beauty it has to share with you. Love is not elusive like the pot of gold at the end of the rainbow. Love is what lies inside of you. Love is the most important thing of creation, for creation is love. When you have found true love within you, share the spark with someone you truly love. So you ask, how will I know if I've found true love? To this I respond, you will see a bright light glowing within you. You will feel completely at one with yourself or in the union with another soul. When two souls that share such a deep level of love and understanding unite, there can be no doubt that you together have found true love.

A rainbow of crystals surrounds you. You are in a paradise filled with love, let there be no doubts. Turn the doubts into little whispers which are carried away by the wind. Let the wind carry your two souls which merge as one; the light within you shines brilliantly.

True love is pure energy, the energy of two joined as one. For in two united as one, you shall find true love. May the feathers of love caress your body, mind, and soul. May the spirit of love shine within you, and may you find the door that leads to true love. (Shamani)

Tell us about the concept of soulmates.

Old souls, wise souls, those souls have traveled eons to a place known only to them. Sharing the same spirit, equal wisdom, equal love. They embody the truth. Like two crickets in the night, their sounds attract each other, bringing them closer.

Soulmates seek eternal life, eternal truth, a destiny so promised by the elders. The wise ones have joined, have found the truth, now they share it with us. Embodied in nature, a love so everlasting, broken although strained through time. Challenges abound but the souls are strong.

Visions of the past, visions of the future, joined to form the present. The energy of one, the union of many. Blessed are you who walk together in love and unity, for you cherish the bright light that shines within. Honor thy self, take notice, glorify thyself. Be a symbol to others. The love you share is beyond worldly imagine. Glow like the candle, enumerate visibly for all to see. (Shamani)

How do we know if we've met our true soulmate?

True love, an expression of two souls. Soulmates, like two ships passing in the night, reunited.

A barren landscape you have traveled but now you reach a lush tropical landscape. The differences are like night and day. The barren landscape was full of deception, deceit, lies, emptiness, and pain. You felt alone, without purpose. You always hoped and believed something better lie beyond the horizon. The beautiful dark red and orange sunsets seemed so distant. Would you ever reach them—could you ever embrace the beauty fully? I liken this to relationships both past and present which aren't entirely fulfilling. You know that there is a person out there that you feel at one with. But where is he or she? Will I spend a lifetime or lifetimes looking for him or her?

Now you enter a lush rain forest filled with an abundance of life and beauty. You are completely at one and at peace with your surroundings. You never realized such beauty and warmth existed. It is beyond your wildest dreams. Dreams can come true and soulmates do exist. For every half, there is another half. Together, the two halves make a whole. So I say, when you meet your soulmate, you will see a lush rain forest of emotions, ideas, thoughts, and physicality wrapped up in one. You will see yourself in this person but you will also see differences. You have traveled different but similar paths.

Above all, you will feel a love so special and so unique, a love like no other. (Asmuth)

Chapter 5:
Answers About Sexuality

Sexuality, one of the most controversial issues on the earth plane at this time. Male versus female, who is right and who is wrong? Lines of division drawn between the two sexes. Is sex really the issue or is the issue your own insecurity with your own sexual identity? Are you looking for the answers? Well look no further than these pages. I trust that you are willing to accept the truth. Male and female, black and white, red and yellow—there is no difference.

Sexuality is the foundation of who you are. Your soul consists of both male and female energy. A difficult concept for you to understand? Now that I have planted the seed of truth in your mind, the magic of love can be born from the seed.

Love yourself, love another, come together and join as one. The ecstasy—a beautiful fountain, a rainbow of colors anoint you. Your soul spirals out of control but in a positive direction. The direction your soul takes is toward total and pure love. When two souls join as one in love, whether it be physical, mental, and/or spiritual, there is an awareness of another dimension.

Pick a star in the night sky. You can see the star, but there lies a great distance between you and the star. Now, think of reaching that star as being the ultimate sexual experience. But, remember each of you will see the star differently and visualize what it will be like when you reach the star. Others of you may see the star as being too distant and unreachable. But for those of you who reach the star, you will experience the ultimate climax, way beyond your wildest dreams.

So, as you set a course for the star, read the words that follow to assist you along your journey. May your journey be a safe and responsible one. (Asmuth)

What meaning does sexuality bring to our lives?

Oh violets so plentiful in the garden of paradise, from whence we came. Oh to share such beautiful things. The stars glisten in the nighttime sky. Roses blossoming in the sunlight, oh silent beams of pleasure. See through distant starlit skies, to a new paradise, a paradise of love and sharing. Only when two are joined can such pleasure be paramount.

A garden of blossoms from which all life comes. Sensations abound, glistening like starlight in a twilight sky. Roses purport the knowledge. Each bloom, each petal unfolds divinely. True love abounds in the union of two, joined in ecstasy. Sexuality takes many forms, like colors of the rainbow. Bright blue, the sphinx, the keeper of the secret of life, long withstanding. (Asmuth)

What would you say to someone who is having difficulty accepting his or her own sexual identity?

I see a person chained to the walls of inadequacy. I also see a valley filled with orange, yellow, red, and green colored trees. The different colors represent the different parts of that person's feelings.

Do you feel anger or joy? Are you comfortable with who you are? If you are not sure, stand in front of a mirror and ask yourself, who am I? Only you can answer this question.

So often I see many of you looking outside of yourselves to gain a sense of your identity. The best gift you can give yourself is to be true to yourself. If you run away from who you are or play games with other people, you only deny yourself. Opportunities await, once you open yourself. Deal with your emotions whether they be love, anger, rage, hate, jealousy, or mistrust. Life waits for no one, don't let life pass you by.

Face your demons, the creations of your mind. The mental images you have conjured are self-destructive.

Identity is a reality-based, self-serving image. Do not let other people dictate who you are. Let go of the chains that bind you, for when you have your own personal identity, no one can wield power over you. (Asmuth)

Why do we have two, possibly three, sexual identities (male, female energy)?

You are both male and female in the light, the light encompasses all that is, has been, and ever will be. This is the essence of "one." One consists of both male and female energies, both are equal. So, if you have been conceived from one, then your soul consists of both male and female energies. Each of you are both male and female, regardless of the way you perceive maleness and femaleness.

The reason you have male and female sexual identities is so that each of you can experience what it is like to be male and female. Remember that your society draws the distinctions between females and males. Your feelings, thoughts, and ideas of the earth plane are based on these distinctions. Gender equality should not be an issue. When people profess that males and females are not equal, they defile their own existence.

In essence, you all share one sexual identity, that of male-female. If you accept this truth, you will better understand who you are. If you utilize the aspects of your male and female energies equally, you will realize there is no difference. For in the union of male and female energy, you are one. (Asmuth)

Why do we need sexual release?

Sexual release is a form of healing. Through sexual release, the mind, body, and spirit are brought into balance. Balance is an essential component of your well-being. Sexual release is an expression of your spirit and your spirit must be freely and creatively expressed.

Remember that everything is composed of energy. Your thoughts of love, either of yourself or another person, are transformed into sexual energy. Sexual energy is potent with desire and fills your mind, body, and soul. Sexual energy draws from the other energies inside you. Think of it like a magnet. Have you ever gotten wrapped up in a moment of deep passion? Do you feel in control at this moment? No, all your thoughts and energy are concentrated on sexual passion.

If suddenly you were cut off from the passion, you would feel totally imbalanced. Why? Because now you have an overabundance of sexual energy and no release for it. However, if you continue to build the level of sexual passion, you reach a point of ecstasy and release. When you have sexual release, then you are balanced once again. For some of you though, multiple sexual releases—which you term climaxes or orgasms—are necessary to achieve balance.

Do not deny yourself sexual release, but I also caution you not to seek sexual fulfillment with multiple partners. I ask you to maintain purity (single partners) in your relationships. Sexual release by two souls in love at the same moment can be a divine experience. If you do not have a person to share sexual release with, then find sexual release with yourself. You know what you need and when you need it. I ask you to keep your thoughts pure and simple. There is no need to disrespect or objectify another person or thing for your pleasure. Sexual release can be attained by focusing on pure beauty and love.

Let sexual release be an expression of who you are. Let yourself go, you'll be surprised at the heights you can reach. Be free and creative with yourself and/or the one you love. Unite in ecstasy, for in ecstasy you shall find freedom and balance again. (Shamani)

Why do some people have such strong sexual appetites while others seem to be nonchalant about sex?

The mind, spirit, and body are all connected. Think of each of these as centers. During the act of sex or making love, these centers are opened. All three centers are allowed to unite on one level. For those who can feel this, the act of sex becomes premier in their life. The feelings of love, warmth, peace surround them.

For those who seem to be nonchalant about sex, there is something else which piques their interest. This may be interest in another person or thing. The act of sex for them is not at all what it is to someone who feels the union of body, mind, and spirit. This is not to say that this is bad.

Oftentimes, a person who is nonchalant about sex has no physical or mental desire to explore such realms of love. The reasons may be varied. It may be that the person has an aversion to his or her own sexuality, or possibly a former abusive relationship, or a dysfunctional concept of love. These may also be reasons to explain why certain people have strong sexual appetites. There may be an appetite of the mind, an unquenchable thirst for promiscuity and exhibition.

Whatever the reasons, a strong sexual appetite should not be a substitute for love. Nor should nonchalance be an excuse for what you fear. Is love what you fear? (Asmuth)

Why do we have so much jealousy in love/sexual relationships?

Jealousy, an affliction of the heart. In your love and sexual relationships, you often want to possess and control the one you love. When a relationship is not built on solid trust, you seek other ways to build a foundation of love. Love can not be forced or controlled, it must be freely expressed. Love is an expression of the mind, body, and spirit.

The games of love, I see many of you play. When you don't feel good about yourself, you seek the admiration of another. You look outside yourself for emotional fulfillment.

The games of jealousy used to arouse your partner. Do you expect to evoke and arouse love out of jealousy? Jealousy can hurt and leave scars for many years. Does making another feel jealous gratify you? Does it make you feel better? Again, you look outside yourself for that which you lack. Is what you lack love for yourself?

For those who feel jealous without any just cause, I ask you to examine why you feel jealous. Are you afraid that the person or animal (a pet) will leave you? I ask you to believe in yourself, value yourself, and do not judge yourself.

Jealousy is the color red with envy. Jealousy can only affect you if you feel insecure or inadequate. If you place conditions and expectations on love, then you invite jealousy. Jealousy has no power by itself unless you give it power.

The leaves of gold (love) are not painted with jealousy. (Shamani)

How do we get beyond our own possessive needs in love/sexual relationships?

Listen to the waters of the river. The water moves collectively downstream, sometimes smoothly and sometimes rapidly. The water particles bond together, each particle acts independently, there is no need for possession.

Trust the natural flow of life. Move independently, yet in unison with others. Do not impede your progress or the progress of another. Do not seek to possess another person or thing. Look to the trees, the trees do not possess the leaves and so the leaves fall to the ground. So I say the same should be with you. If the leaves did not fall to the ground, you would not see the birds in the trees or the bare branch. So you see, if you possess someone or something, you will never truly see what lies within that person or thing.

Believe that you have all that you need and share what you have. For in possession, you deny free expression. (Shamani)

Why is fidelity so important to some human beings and seemingly unimportant to others?

Why does the forest appear green to some and brown to others? It is all perception. Words mean different things to each individual. There is power in words, empires have fallen because of words. Relationships fail because of words.

Fidelity has power but only the power that you give it. What is the true purpose for practicing fidelity? Is it a way to control and seduce others? Does everything fit neatly in a box? Of course not, ideas and thoughts are pulled from the ethers at random and given form and expression. Is fidelity an expression of the truth? Not entirely, for those who practice infidelity express the truth also.

On Earth, many of your societies dictate what is right and wrong, and what the truth consists of. How is this determined? Generally by a few select people, then the rest follow. The "truth" is written into history books. These books might be labeled fiction by many who read them.

Fidelity is a control mechanism of the heart (soul). The heart (soul) seeks oneness with another heart (soul). When it finds oneness, it seeks to retain the oneness. Love is the joining of two souls as one.

I ask you not to differentiate fidelity into being important or unimportant. Remember that words are only a manifestation of thoughts. The power you give to words can change the course of time. History is a compilation of words, not necessarily the truth. (Asmuth)

How did the concept of fidelity originate?

Out of love, the seed of fidelity was born. When two souls unite in love, there is peace and balance. A rainbow of colors shine down upon you.

Let no other person divide you (two souls). If the two souls are united in true love, the bond will be unbreakable. However, if one soul wavers and thrashes about, the bond may be broken. One or both of the souls may venture outward to seek that balance once again. It is love the soul seeks. Superficial love can be detrimental to a soul's growth. True love is recognized by the soul.

In the beginning, each soul was taught to honor and love itself. Out of this was born the concept of loyalty. In order to be loyal, you must be true to yourself. When two souls united in something other than true love, the concept of infidelity was born.

There are many levels of love. It is up to you to recognize and understand what level you are on with each person and thing. Do you love nature in the same way as you do your spouse? Do you express your love for each of these in the same way?

Feelings of love must come from the heart (soul). Money and gifts can't buy love. Love is free and you have the freedom to express it.

Remember, infidelity is created when two souls are not embraced in true love. If you honor yourself, then you can be faithful to another. (Asmuth)

How did the concept of adultery originate?

Purple beams of passion, from a seed, a thought was born. Many see the purple beams of passion enticing. Adultery is an age-old concept. The term (adultery) you use disturbs me, I see so much negative energy radiating from it. I see mixed emotions, those of love, pain, guilt, and jealousy.

The concept of adultery originated at a time when love was free and uninhibited. Each soul was free to love another. But there came a time when one soul wanted to control the soul of another. Many souls were cast aside. The value of love was diminished. Love became a tool of control and imprisonment of many souls (people).

If there is true love between two souls, there can be no adultery. The love shared by two souls stands true in the light. In this instance, adultery does not exist. (Asmuth)

What would you say to someone whose partner has been "unfaithful"?

You must look at your reflection in a pool. What do you see? Are you to blame for this? I hear your cries of passion and pain. But to you I say, do not cast stones at another. Love takes many forms, it can be molded but will it necessarily remain in that shape? The love between two souls must continue to grow. Love and growth depend on each other. Without love, there is no growth, and without growth, there is no love. By this, I mean a deep shared love. Simple "I love you's" are only words from the mind and not an expression of the heart.

You whose partner has been "unfaithful" could find a thousand reasons to blame yourself, your partner, and the other people involved. As much pain as you feel, try to understand and respect your partner's life path. I know it is not easy, the pain runs deep.

You can either choose to let this destroy you or help you to grow. True love must be free of games of the mind and heart. Love cannot be a controlled emotion nor can you use it to control others.

There are no simple answers or consolations I can offer. Each individual must search their own soul and bring out a ball of glowing love. Hold the love in your hands and share it. (Asmuth)

Are we heterosexual by nature?

Each individual is a reflection of himself or herself. Heterosexual is a word which you (collectively) use to control and categorize men and women into groups of males and females. As I have said, each individual is composed of male and female energies. Your individual identity is drawn from the combination of these energies. Both male and female energies are equal in form but not in expression.

And so I say, why do many of you deny an individual's free expression of their own gender identity? The stones you cast at others are often the stones of inadequacy and insecurity. The terms heterosexual and homosexual have no basis in truth. These terms are only used to separate you from each other. If you could see only the soul, would such a label make sense?

The delegates of wisdom open the gates to freedom. They ask you to respect each other's right to free expression.

Watch in wonder, the glorious creation—that which is you. Seek to unite as one, do not seek discord through labels. Remember from one you were conceived, to one you shall return. But, each of you has the freedom to express your individual spirit. Let your individual spirit be truly representative of who you are.

So you ask, are you heterosexual by nature? To this I say, you are all one by nature but you are also individual expressions of spirit. (Asmuth)

Do heterosexual and homosexual partners experience sexuality differently?

If sexuality is based on love, there can be no difference. Man to man, man to woman, woman to man, or woman to woman—if two souls are connected in love, there is no difference. I ask you to remember that each and every one of you consists of both male and female energies.

Whether you have chosen to incarnate on Earth as a female or male makes no difference. The differences you perceive only serve to separate you from love and yourself. If you believe we are all conceived from and return to "the essence of one," then why admonish others for their choices.

The choice of a "man" to be with a "man" is the same as the choice of a "woman" to be with a "woman," a "man" to be with a "woman," and a "woman" to be with a "man." Love knows no boundaries, only the boundaries of love and hate that you support. But I remind you that you can choose to accept your femaleness and maleness. By doing so, you will surely be able to accept other people's choices for sexual partners. Where there is love, there is acceptance.

Sexual relations between two partners should be based on an intimate sharing of love. Sex for the sake of sex may fulfill your mental and physical desires, but it leaves a deep void in your soul. I ask you to discover new ways to arouse and entice your partner. Love can be shared in a multitude of ways and on a multitude of levels.

Open yourself to the many possibilities of love on a higher plane. Surround yourself with love and create your own personal guide to lovemaking. Focus on allowing your female and male energies to coexist in balance with your body, mind, and spirit.

Allow yourself to express love and sexuality in both a non-heterophobic and non-homophobic manner. If you perceive no difference in sexuality and love, then there will be none. (Shamani)

Why do so many people engage in "kinky" and sometimes harmful sexual acts?

Those who engage in such acts seek gratification. The act of sex in such a provocative manner gives them a sense of power. Control over another person or thing is a common theme. Themes from movies, abolitions of the heart acted out in human form. The images they see are comparable to dungeons and dragons. Oh, the dragon slayer engaged in such acts just before he slew the dragon.

Sex for some is an act, some type of theatre. They do not see the people they engage in "kinky" sex with as being real. It is almost as if they see right through them—they do not recognize the person or thing.

Through force and control, these people feel a false sense of power over their "subject." They experience a high level of emotion during the sexual act. It is like a drug to them.

Through the body, they try to attain a perpetual state of mental stimulation. (Asmuth)

Why do we have orgasmic feelings?

An orgasm is a magical expression of love. Orgasmic feelings are like a dormant volcano which erupts with fire and ash. The fire is red with passion, the ash is symbolic of the physical release. The passion and release are an expression of self-love. At the point of orgasm, you are truly out of your body, surrounded by love.

A rainbow of ecstasy is created out of the fountain of love. The fountain is an endless stream. To this end, your orgasms are only limited by your feelings of love.

Your orgasms take you to the heights of ecstasy. In those moments, you are flying, your spirit soars.

You have orgasmic feelings so that you may feel the freedom of love. Love is a personal and individual expression of your mind, body, and spirit. Orgasmic feelings allow you to reach the greatest heights in yourself. The greatest heights are those of unconditional love for yourself.

I ask you to go within yourself and release the purple passion that lies within you. Soar to the heights of ecstasy and embody what your orgasm symbolizes—a free expression of love. (Asmuth)

What is the ultimate sexual experience?

You rejoice too soon, keep on giving. Maintain a continuous stream of love. Give of yourself entirely to the person you love. Capture the moment and become one with the moment of ecstasy. Do not restrict yourself. When you become one with the moment, you will become one with the light. To me, this is the ultimate sexual experience.

But some of you may ask, how does it feel? Think of being surrounded by all the love in the universe—a universal climax. Bathe yourself in love, feel the peace and joy. You not only feel it, but you are also one with it. Visualize yourself in a garden paradise surrounded by flowers of every conceivable color. Think of the peace and joy you feel in these surroundings.

Visualize what it is like to be one of those flowers surrounded by an innumerable amount of flowers. Look at yourself in the garden, what do you see? Can you describe the feelings you have? Your feelings actually defy description, for you are one with the flower, one with your feelings.

The flower breathes, visualize puffs of air emerging from the petals. The essence of who you are is in each puff of air, and each one surrounds you. The individual puffs of air combine and form a bubble. The bubble keeps growing until it reaches a bursting point. At this point, all the air and energy—the essence of who you are—is released around you. You bask in the energy that completely surrounds you. The energy consists of your mental, physical, and spiritual energies, a unique blend of all that you are.

So you see, the ultimate sexual experience can only be found within you. You are the creator of your own sexual identity and feelings. The ultimate sexual experience is based on love, the love that lies within you. When you conceive of love, you will become one with love. For love is the essence of who you are. You are the ultimate sexual experience. (Shamani)

Part III:
Answers for All of Us

Chapter 6:
Answers About the Family

Welcome to the universal family, you are not alone. In the beginning, a child was born of two parents: the essence of female and the essence of male. Conceived from the light of the spirit, a family was born. The child spirit was completely positive and completely surrounded by love. From a spirit of true love, all others were conceived.

Think of a feather gently caressing your face, much like a baby's breath. The naiveté and the innocence of birth and the young. The child grows to be an adolescent, a young adult, an adult, and finally an elder. Do wisdom and knowledge make us stronger? Is our family enriched by the beauty and love we have and share for each other?

Questions and answers about the family, why have we all come together? We are all beings of light with different personalities yet we are all connected. How can this be, you ask? Soon you shall know, but until you transform knowledge into awareness and wisdom, you shall only know what someone else has told you. So, as you read this chapter, ponder the question: what does the word "family" mean to me? Is it just a word or do you truly feel part of a family?

Many of you seem to think that family values are a thing of the past. But, you can revive the concept of a family by loving all things in the universal family. Remember we are all one. You may encounter difficulties with certain members of our family. I ask you to project feelings and thoughts of love, peace, and harmony toward that person or thing. Have patience with one another and above all love and respect one another.

We all share one universe, so let us join as one family in love. (Shamani)

Why do we come together—on this plane—in family or cohabitational units (communities)?

Like feathers floating through the air, they find a place to call home. So too do we yearn for that place, a place to join others on a similar life path. To share the wind's whispers, the gathering of ideas presented in a forum.

Snowflakes accumulate with like snowflakes, although different sizes and shapes, fit perfectly. So too it is with the family, collective souls joined to share life's truths. The journey may be arduous and long but the benefits are rewarding. Cataclysmic events can be endured with a love of the heart. Perpetual forgiveness may be sought. Divine guidance is often necessary to traverse troubled waters.

The glistening howl of the coyote symbolizes the call of a new day, reborn of the spirit, devoid of doubt. Bring forth your brothers and sisters, bring them into the light of day. Choose a path, a path of fortitude, a place to call home. Live within your means, and create a means to an end.

Struggles are on the forefront, destitute mothers, fathers who know not what to do. Plant a seed and watch it grow. From that seed, a family may be born. Birth, the giver of life.

Cloudless skies, catch a rainbow, the gold awaits in all its grandeur. That elusive pot of gold, it is there, if only in your mind's eye. Eyes, the windows of the soul, the keeper of legend. The legend of a man's journey, the journey to oblivion. He went there and came back to tell all that he saw. But no one believed him, so a legend was born out of truth and not belief. So it is with you, I tell you, believe in yourself. For you are the truth and the light.

Wisdom comes to all who seek it. Forsake those who cross your path, there are windows that can be opened. Do not mock them, all who come to hear you come with their own set of eyes. They see what they want to see. In all their glory, they have a purpose. A purpose to be fulfilled, a cape to put on to mask their own truth. A masquerade ball of the heart, so serene and so deceitful that no one knows how to read it. To this I say, read only what you can see and cast out what you can not.

The altar lies before you, a symbol of two points meeting (a cross). If two life paths cross, then share the journey and honor the other person's life path. Respond in kindness. (Shamani)

How can parents and children improve their relationships?

Build a bridge together and meet in the middle. The river divides you but the bridge shall bring you together. Cast your doubts, fears, anger, and mistrust into the waters below. The currents shall carry them away.

Hug each other, become close again. Embrace each other's ideas. You'll be surprised how much you have in common. There is a common link that binds you. You were brought together for a reason. The reasons are not always clear.

Be sincere in your gestures of good faith. Communicate your differences. If something is bothering you, speak up. No one can hear your silence.

Relationships are built upon love. Is this not what brought you together? Love is not an abstract idea. It is one on one, an expression of each other unified as one. Speak kindly to each other, kind words are often what was lacking previously.

Respect each other's life path and purpose. Celebrate the differences between you. Share ideas and concepts—listen to one another. Be open to new ideas. Challenge yourself to improve the relationship.

We can sit around and talk about what we envision as a perfect relationship. But there comes a time when we must do something about it. Fantasies never become reality, until we act upon them.

No matter what has divided you in the past, there is one thing you can find in the other person that is good. Take that one thing and build upon it. Once the seed of love is planted, it can't help but grow. Your relationship can be as beautiful as pink, red, and white cherry blossoms in the spring. The choice is yours. (Asmuth)

How can we become less critical of others?

Your criticism of others is based on that which you do not like in yourself. You must acknowledge and understand this simple truth first. The road to forgiveness is often paved with reflections of yourself.

It is easy to be critical of others, most often you need someone to blame for your choices. If you have high expectations of yourself and others, you are more prone to be the subject and object of criticism. For that which you give, you get back.

If others met your expectations, would you be less critical of them? Of yourself? Expectations are only good for the person who creates them. By good I mean the expectations fit perfectly for that person. But I ask you to realize that each one of you has different expectations.

If you would like to become less critical of others, then identify what you do not like in yourself. Many of you try to find security in money. Most often, if you feel you do not have an abundance of money, you are critical of others who seemingly have an abundance of money. The reason you are critical of others is that you are insecure with the amount of money you have.

I give you another example. You are in a place where there is a lot of noise. You expected that this place would be peaceful. Your expectations have not been met, so you become critical of others. I ask you to see this as a lesson in balance. Ultimately, you can find peace in noise. If you are uncomfortable in a situation, then remove yourself from it. Before you criticize other people and things, try to understand both extremes (peace and noise). Some people enjoy peace and quiet while others relish loudness. There is a time and place for each.

Ultimately, you must learn to accept each other's life paths. For some of you, the path to the truth is disguised in noise, and for others, the truth is disguised in peace and quiet. Learn to respect each person and thing. The bird in the tree has as equal a right to life on the earth plane as you.

You can learn much from the other inhabitants of the earth (the plants, trees, insects, and rocks). Ask yourself, are the plants, trees, birds, insects, and rocks critical of each other? No. Why, you ask? Because they respect each other.

It only takes one of you to initiate criticism of another. Break the cycle of criticism and replace your critical thoughts with thoughts of love. Learn to love the reflection of yourself in another person. (Asmuth)

How can we help our children develop a good self-image?

Help them to develop themselves. Allow them to develop their own self-identity. Nurture that spark or glow that lies within them.

Allow them to be independent, do not control them. Control of your children diminishes the potential which lies within each one of them. Children will make mistakes along the way, we all do from time to time.

Give them mental exercises to do. Give them a rose or another object, have them describe it, then have them compare its qualities to themselves. You will also find out how your children view themselves.

Give them responsibility, a little at a time. By allowing them to be responsible for their actions, they will see the consequences of their actions. This will help them develop a good self-image.

Love your children and allow them to love you. Love is the center of all things. Show them you care, not just on the surface, but deep down in your heart.

Encourage your children, applaud their merits. Everyone needs to feel appreciated and loved. Always strive to do your best, the best lies within each of you.

Teach your children kindness. Kindness can be far-reaching, even a simple hello or thank you can make a difference in someone's day. Through kindness to ourselves and others, we develop a better self-image.

Reinforce these ideas and most of all, let the concept of individuality remain at the forefront in your child's development.

Though individually we grow, collectively we prosper. (Asmuth)

How can we become better listeners?

When an acorn drops from a tree in the forest and no one is there, does anyone hear it? An abstract thought, I grant you, but there is truth in what I say. If no one listened to what I say, all of what I say would fall on deaf ears.

Listen to the whispers of nature. Take a moment to become still and listen to all the sounds around you. So much of your lives are consumed with sound (the sound of your vehicles, radios, televisions, and conversations). How much do you really listen to and absorb? How much goes in one ear and out the other? How much falls on deaf ears? You must ask yourself these questions.

By being more aware of your surroundings, you will develop a greater sense of what is really important. Take time to go within and listen to yourself. What does your "heart" tell you?

Allow peace and tranquillity into your life. If you constantly surround yourself with noise, you will never hear yourself. Stop running, take a moment to be with yourself, and just listen. (Shamani)

How can we help our children feel a sense of belonging?

Dreams. Teach them to dream. Relish the thoughts of eternal destiny.

Encourage them, nurture them, bring them a new set of ideals. See each day as a bright new day.

Bring out the spark in each child—the thing that makes them happy. Nurture that aspect of them. (Asmuth)

How can we help our children during adolescence?

There can never be a substitute for love. Respect and honor your child's life path. During the period of adolescence, the fabric of your child will be challenged. The child faces many challenges, some easy and some difficult. The difficulty lies in how the child deals with the problems he or she encounters. There may be encounters with the deep, dark side of themselves. You must let them fall and get back up again.

The children are well-guided and protected. But, they must open themselves. Only those who look up can see the birds in the sky. Remember the mother bird must watch as her fledglings try to fly from the nest. She must believe instinctually that the young birds will take up flight.

So the same should be with parents. Your children will fall but they must get back up on their own. The greatest gift you can give your child is independence. Help them to foster independent thinking and reasoning abilities. Share your thoughts and abilities with them. Teach them the way of the warrior and the peacemaker. Let them make their own choices but guide them along the way.

Remember, you were an adolescent at one time. You had feelings, thoughts, and urges that seemed foreign to you. Use what you have learned and share your wisdom with your child. Also, remember that through love and understanding, all things are possible.

Be a friend to your child. It is important for a child to know that you are someone they can confide in. Help your child to understand this stage in their life.

Encourage them to embrace love and life. In turn, embrace and hug your child. Teach them to trust the natural flow of life and to seek the truth.

Nurture their need to find their own identity. Do not place value judgments on them or their actions. You may not agree with what they do but I ask you to honor and respect their decisions. Decisions, whether "right" or "wrong," foster learning and growth. See that it is important to grow with your adolescent child, instead of away from him or her. (Shamani)

Why is it difficult for many fathers and sons to get along?

One mountain is higher than the other. The smaller mountain will never measure up to the grandest mountain. The smaller mountain feels inferior. The taller mountain seemingly speaks down to the smaller mountain.

The son does not realize that it took a long time for the father to grow that tall. The son wishes he could be like his father. I say, no matter how hard you try, you (the son) will never be like your father. You are your own being, an individual, custom-designed.

Egos, power struggles, competition—who can reach the highest point? When the son is young, the father always seems to win at everything. But as the father gets older, the son soon finds he can win at some things. But no matter how old the son gets, he will never have the wisdom of his father. There is a balance which can be attained. Do you wish to find that balance? (Asmuth)

Why is it difficult for many mothers and daughters to get along?

The two rams lock their horns. They step back and face off again. Although they are of the same family, they compete for food, territory, and love. Soon they tire of this endless battle and one retreats. They both go their separate ways, find a place to lay down, and think.

For mothers and daughters, this analogy fits. Differences in opinions, ideas, feelings—who is right? You or I?

Differences of heart, this is what I see. But you must ask yourself, do I love myself? If you do, then celebrate your differences. There is no need for argument. The purple flower is a symbol of healing. Heal the wounds. It is all right to have a difference in opinion, it is what makes us individuals. Individual thoughts and actions unite us as a whole.

Find that which you do not like in yourself. It is often what we see in others that we do not like in ourselves. Celebrate the self.

Why do two female cats taunt and fight each other? One cat is aggressive while the other is non-aggressive. The aggressive cat is possessive and feels the need to stake out a territory, an area to exercise power and dominion over, while the non-aggressive cat wishes not to fight but to stand firm. Aggression vs. non-aggression, where is the boundary line? Who is right? In your mind, you may say that the aggressive cat is wrong. But then you are influenced by your idea of aggression and your ideas of right and wrong.

I say to you, try not to find fault in yourself or others. It is a fine line to walk and not very easy to do. Stand firm, for what you believe is right. But also acknowledge another's right to do the same. (Shamani)

How can we nurture our own self-esteem as well as that of others?

Build a monument of love to yourself. Love is the greatest healer. When you feel good about yourself, you love yourself, and when you love yourself, you feel good about yourself. So you see, love and self-esteem walk hand in hand.

I ask you to believe in yourself also. You are only limited by your beliefs. If you believe in success, then success you shall embrace. There is nothing you can't do, your mind is a very powerful tool and often underutilized. The power of love will help heal the scars of the past. The scars are symbolic of your "failures" as a person. But, I ask you not to view your life as a "failure," remember that you only "failed" to realize your own potential. There is so much good that lies within you, if only you take the time to become one with yourself.

Feel good about yourself. I ask you to think about one thing today that you felt good about. Take that feeling and build upon it. Build a foundation of love and on top of that love, build a structured network of self-esteem. Each time you feel good, take that feeling and add it to the network. Always remind yourself to keep adding to the network.

In order to nurture self-esteem in others, you must first develop self-esteem in yourself. Share the information I have given to you. By sharing how good you feel with others, you will build a universal network of self-esteem. Remember that all of you are full of love, allow yourself to express it. If you learn to love yourself and others, self-esteem will flow naturally within you. (Asmuth)

What do you think about adoption?

Adoption is truly a blessing for the adopted child and family. There is a balance of love here which is so necessary. The magical bond between a child and parent can never be broken. Adoption creates opportunities for growth for all of those involved in the adoption process. Once the adoption is final, a new family is created. A sense of security and stability is once again re-established in the minds of the child and parents.

Peace and prosperity fill the hearts of those who are willing to give the gift of life. It is not so important that you bear a child but what you give that child after it is born. Many of you forget this. Conceiving the child is the easy part, raising the child properly in a warm and loving environment is more challenging. Every one of you is capable of both giving and receiving love.

If you are willing to adopt a child, or even an animal or a tree, be prepared to accept the responsibility of properly caring for them. Whether an infant or adolescent, both require a lot of love. Spend time with your child and if they ask questions about their adoption, be honest with them. The skies may not always shine brightly and you may have to weather storms of emotion. But remember who and what you are. You have given life to someone who so richly deserves it.

Always remember that there are many children who may never be adopted. If you choose not to adopt a child, then support the people that do. Remember them in your meditations and prayers. Send them an abundance of love. You have a family, now think what you would feel like if you never had a mother or father. Always count your blessings, for there are many who have far less than you. No matter how much or how little you have, you always have yourself. (Asmuth)

What would you say to those who have been adopted?

The magician uses many tools to produce an illusion. Is your life mired in illusion? Do you see your adopted parents as not being your "real" parents? There could be nothing farther from the truth. Your parents are those you have chosen for this lifetime. As difficult as this may be for you to accept, it is the truth.

When you were a baby or child, a decision was made by your mother and/or father to give you up for adoption, in hopes that another family could provide you with love and understanding.

For whatever reasons, your mother and father chose to give you "a better life." They may have regretted the decision then or later on.

The important thing to remember is that you were conceived in love. You may not remember those who conceived you, but they surely remember you. The memory of a baby is forever ingrained in their hearts. They think of you often and wonder what might have been. In their soul, they did what was just and right at the time. They gave you a new lease on life. Now, you must honor what you have been given.

Your true parents are those who have unselfishly given their life to make a life for you. So I ask you to honor, love, and respect them. Do not find fault with them. For if you do, you only find fault with yourself. Love is the most beautiful and plentiful feeling in the world. You are surrounded by love each and every day. I ask you to recognize what you have.

If you dwell in the past, you will surely stagnate. Remember, you have chosen a seemingly more difficult path than others. Be assured that an abundance of love surrounds you, if you are only willing to accept it.

Acceptance is your most important lesson. You can choose to remain mired in illusion or you can look in the mirror and say, "I love you, Mom and Dad." (Asmuth)

What would you say to the parents of a "handicapped" child?

To each end, there is a new beginning. I can sense that your heart and mind are worn from the journey. But I ask you to be strong. Your child needs you and you need your child. Together, you give each other strength and courage. It takes a lot of courage to stand in the light and "see" the truth. This applies both to the child and parents.

Do not punish or blame yourself as parents. The life lessons we choose are often riddles of mystery. But, if you can solve the riddle or mystery, then you have mastered the lesson. In order to master the lesson, you must first understand what you have chosen to learn. Some of your most difficult lessons are disguised in fear. You fear what you do not understand. I ask you to face your fear. Fear enslaves you, but you can escape. How, you ask? To this I say, love comes in small packages. It is up to you to open the package and realize the great gift you have been given. A child is the greatest gift of all, he or she is a creation of two souls united in love.

No child is "handicapped." Often the people who see someone as "handicapped" are handicapped themselves. Their handicap is guilt, anger, and fear. They mask their insecurity and judgments in these three feelings.

Your child is much more evolved in mind, body, and spirit than you might perceive. Your child has unlimited potential—nurture that potential. Teach yourself and your child that the beauty of love is not limited to the physical body. The body is only a shell for your soul. The soul is truly beautiful and defies judgment.

Love the child you have been given, for the miracle of creation is truly a miracle of love. (Shamani)

How can people deal with dependency issues?

Dependency is that which keeps you a slave to yourself. The issue is not dependency itself, but what type of behavior in you facilitates dependency. In order to deal with dependency issues, you (people) must identify the behaviors in you which create patterns of dependency. Do you not trust the ground you walk on? Do you let anger, depression, and fear control you? In essence, you become dependent on these feelings of inadequacy and insecurity. Your learned behaviors foster dependency.

I ask you to believe that you have all the abundance you need. The universe will provide for you, but not in a dependent way.

The universe will give you what you need, it is up to you to use it wisely.

Think of yourself as a fabric woven of dependence and independence. Each thread of you is independent from the other, but all the threads are dependent on each other to keep you together. Each thread has its own purpose. Each thread is strong. When the threads are woven together, purpose is dependent on strength and strength is dependent on purpose. You see, there is a balance. Both strength and purpose, and dependence and independence, are equal. So, I ask you to find both strength and purpose in dependence and independence. Do not be a slave to either.

If you erect a fence or fortress around yourself, you will always be dependent on yourself and others. When you open the gates and venture outside the walls of dependency, you will find the truth that will set you free from dependency. You will see that dependence and independence can walk hand in hand in your life. (Shamani)

What do we learn from being children?

You learn the power of love in all its innocence. As a child, you are a symbol of innocence. Being a child allows you to freely express love. Love is the center of your being, you were created out of love. As a child, you learn the healing power of love. Love is often based on faith and belief in yourself.

The bells chime to signal the birth of a child. The purple fruit of passion is passed from hand to hand. All who witness the birth rejoice in the creation. For the baby is a symbol of love in its most precious form. Isn't childhood what many of you return to during the middle of your life?

If you could only remember the moment of your conception, both on the earth plane and at the beginning of life. You were conceived in the brightest beam of light. The light was not blinding, but very comforting. The warmth you felt came from the enormous love that surrounded you. You were aware of everything around you and yet you were at peace.

When you incarnated onto the earth plane, you had a complete memory of your conception. As time progressed and as your soul settled into the earth plane, your memories of conception faded. But as a child, adolescent, and adult, you still retain some memory though it is repressed. It can be likened to having a vision, thought, or idea in your mind, then losing it. The vision, thought, or idea is still there in your mind, but you can't easily recall it.

Being a child teaches you many things. One of these things is the natural progression of learning. Learning takes place in stages. Why, you ask? So that you may survive. You, like all animals, are born with instincts. Instincts are necessary for survival. As an example, a fish stays in the water because it "knows" that it can't survive on land. But, did the fish always know this or did it learn this from its ancestors? The truth is the fish learned to stay in the water from its ancestors. As I said, learning takes place in stages. In every stage, there is a natural progression or order. As a child, you build upon that which you have learned previously, both earlier in this life as well as in past lives.

As a child, many ideas and concepts are forced upon you. But you have the ultimate choice whether to accept or reject the ideas or concepts. Through the choices you make, you develop a sense of who you are—your identity. As you become stronger in your identity, the choices become easier. Also, as a child, your thoughts and feelings are challenged. Challenges make you stronger, though at times you feel weaker.

Most importantly, as a child, you learn to be yourself. You are a free expression of love in its most innocent form. You embody what many adult souls wish to return to.

I ask you (adults) to remember where you came from. You were and always will be a purple fruit of passion (a child). From love you were conceived. Remember, the love that surrounded you at your point of conception is not a distant memory. The child inside of you never dies, it is forever reborn. (Asmuth)

What do we learn from being parents?

Parents, you are a reflection of your children. For you were once children. As a child, you looked to your parents for love, guidance, answers, and care. Parents are the providers, you provide what your child needs to function as an adult. It is a big responsibility which many of you do not realize. When you bring a life into this world, it is your responsibility to provide that child with love. Love cannot be selfish, it must be shared. And this you must teach your children.

So many of you are still children, yet you are parents. What happens when you put two children together? You know what I speak of. Most often, two children (adolescents) conceive a child. Remember what I said about what you learn from being a child. You might re-read the information I gave you. There is much truth in it.

Pay close attention to what I say about learning taking place in stages, following a natural progression. You must always build on what you have learned previously. If you take shortcuts in your life, you will only return to the lessons that you have skipped. This is a simple truth which I place in a language which you can understand.

As parents, you have the opportunity to share the wisdom and knowledge you have acquired. Wisdom, knowledge, and love are the greatest gifts you can give your children. What you give your children will be passed on to their children, and so on. So, I ask you to be careful with your gifts, know that what you are giving your children is the truth. The truth is that which can stand in the light.

Be a symbol of love and truth for your children. Guide them along their chosen life path. Respect their choices and teach them the power of love.

Remember, in this life, you have been both a child and a parent. The cycle of life will continue. You as a parent will be a reflection of your child, and your child will be a reflection of you. (Asmuth)

What can we learn from our grandparents?

Like the elders of the tribe, wisdom is passed down to the young. Those who listen will prosper from the words. The ancient wisdom and teachings give us hope for today as well as tomorrow. The eldest trees in the forest hold the secrets of life. They have seen, they are the visionaries of the past. If you are silent and listen, you can hear them speak.

So I say, it is the same with your grandparents. Go to them with questions. They do not know everything, but what they do know, they will be willing to share.

You who are midway between youth and old age are very fortunate. You have the energy and vibrancy of youth and the wisdom of old age. It is like being on an accelerated path, but only if you are aware of it.

There are many books in the library, all the resources you'll ever need. But, unless you are aware of them and use them, the ideas lay dormant.

Again in middle age, you can see where you've come from (youth) and where you are going (old age). You have the option of not making the same mistakes as your elders and at the same time learning from the mistakes of your youth.

You, one day, will be one of the elders. When you reach that point, may you share the wisdom and embrace the future. (Shamani)

Chapter 7:
Answers About Success

Was I successful, am I successful, or will I be successful? Many of you ask these questions. As you can see, the idea of success can be viewed in terms of the past, present, or future. Which of these three stages are you living in now?

Do you measure success in life by amassing great amounts of financial wealth or spiritual wealth? Is wealth indicative of success? Can an impoverished person never enjoy success? Some of you would say yes, as you throw a few coins in their hand. I will tell you that the poorest, as you see them, are often the most successful. For what they lack in money and material possessions, they make up for in spiritual, mental, and physical abundance.

What does money buy you—a nice house, a nice car or other mode of travel, nice clothes, and people? Yes, I said people. People to do the things you don't want to do or don't have time for. The more people you buy, the more successful you feel.

Where does success come from? Is it something you inherit or learn on your own? Success can only be measured by and for the individual. The development of self-confidence, self-esteem, and self-identity are the keys to each individual's success. Careers may come and go, but the essence of who you are stays the same. I ask you one simple question, do you enjoy and love your job(s), your career, and your life, or are you living a lie to mask your true self?

As you read the questions and answers that follow, develop a sense of who you are and what you are doing with your life. The masquerade can only last one night, for when you see the light of day, you must see who you truly are. When you can see yourself for who you truly are, then and only then will you truly be successful. (Asmuth)

What do we learn from our jobs?

Your job is a reflection of who you are. As a child, the world offers you so many options. You feel like you can do any job you want. This is true—you can be anything you want. But many of you are placed into categories by others who think they know what is best for you. Many of you are labeled privileged or underprivileged children. These labels only serve to separate all of you. I say to you, every child is privileged, every child has the right of free and creative expression. All children should be viewed as equal. And so the same applies to jobs. All jobs are equal. No one job is more important than another.

A job should be something you enjoy doing. Pulling weeds out of a garden can be humbling and enjoyable. Simplicity can be found in almost any action.

Jobs teach you responsibility from the time you are a child caring for yourself to the time you leave the earth plane. Jobs are an outlet for your creative energy and a manifestation of your spirit.

Your jobs are filled with life lessons. Most often, your most difficult and challenging lessons can be found in your work (job). You often expect to get paid for your work in the form of green pieces of paper (money). So I ask you—where do your most difficult and challenging lessons lie? In money, of course. Your job teaches you how to deal with the issue of money and material possessions.

Many of you value yourself by the job you have. Do you really enjoy what you are doing or is it a substitute for something you lack? Is what you lack self-esteem and self-confidence? Again, it goes back to childhood and adolescence, when you were categorized and denied free and creative expression. There is no need to blame yourself or anyone else. The important thing is that you are aware. Once you are aware, you can either accept or change your job(s).

Your job should be a labor of love. For when you love what you are doing, it is not a job. And this I say is what you can learn from your jobs. (Asmuth)

Why do we feel compelled to acquire so many material possessions?

You seek material possessions to patch the holes in your heart. Material possessions disguise your true feelings. Feelings of loneliness are replaced by feelings of ownership. The things you "own" allow you to wear many disguises. You mask your feelings of insecurity with objects of false security. The things you buy or acquire are no substitute for love.

You build a wall of insecurity around yourself. The wall gets higher with each newly acquired material possession. You might think you are happy, but what if you were stripped of all your material possessions, would you still be happy? Could you stand on your own?

The road to happiness is paved with gold. The gold is not for you to acquire, but for you to admire. Everything has a purpose, through awareness you will understand the purpose.

Simplicity is divine. Think of what you have, when you come into this life and when you leave this life. You have your soul. Is your soul a physical thing—something you would readily buy or sell? Your soul belongs to you and you are all you need. (Asmuth)

How much time should we spend working?

I give you gifts to help you make your wayward journey toward peace. Many of you are traveling the road to peace, but few of you recognize the true power of peace. The greatest wars cannot stand in the way of peace. Your world wars are a testament to that. Peace is not for the weak but for the strong.

Working toward peace, in your life and in the world in which you live, should be your primary focus. Battling each other is a form of barbarism. Is the legacy of battle, blood, and pain what you want to leave your children? I ask that you consider the life of every thing as important as your own.

Peace can bring prosperity in the face of poverty. There can be no greater peace than that struck between all citizens of the world. If you work together toward peace, then peace of mind you shall have. Does not your mind grow weary with thoughts of war day in and day out? Does war strengthen your spirit? No, it only weakens it. But the spirit of peace shall forever strengthen you. So, I ask you to affirm peace in every aspect of your life. If you do, you will see positive results. I will caution you that there will always be challenges, but you will always find a peaceful resolution.

Now I shall answer the second part of the question, what many of you thought the question referred to. Do you see your job, career, and lifestyle as work? Does work define your existence? Probabilities and possibilities define your day-to-day life. Life as you know it is a series of hurdles, jumps, and mazes. But, can you find order in all of this confusion? Do you see a light at the end of the tunnel?

Whether you are working at something you love or hate, it is important to take time for yourself. I speak of quiet time, taking time to meditate is one example. The time you spend with yourself is as important as the time you spend working. If you can merge the two, then you will surely be enriched.

You must relax your mind, body, and spirit. Balancing each is the key to your spiritual growth. For when you have balanced each, you can merge them as one. Attaining oneness should be your primary focus in life.

Your work should be a reflection of who you are. Be true to yourself. Trying to escape "reality" through work will only bring you closer to the "reality" of yourself. If you are not happy with the type or quality of work you do, seek to change it or the way you look at it.

The fruits of your labor can not be measured in monetary terms alone. The fruits that will give you the most nourishment are those which you produce. Let your work be a fulfillment of your higher purpose. (Asmuth)

How can we find the best job?

By doing what you do best. Let your job be a labor of love.

If you are doing a job you don't really like, you must ask yourself many questions. One of the questions is, why are you working there? Another question is, by working at a job that I really don't like, am I dishonoring myself? Does this job bring out the best or worst in you?

Change is often difficult for many of you. You often resist that which is good for you and for your higher purpose. If you are willing to change, the universe will provide all that you need.

In order to find the best job, you must align yourself with your higher purpose. In order to determine your higher purpose, you must do some "soul-searching." This means you must sit or lay down in a quiet space and go within. For those who are restless souls, this may be difficult. Allow yourself to be still, let your mind drift, and ask for guidance. Ask your higher guides—whether God, guardian angels, spirit guides, or those who watch over you—to align you with your higher purpose.

You must be ready to accept guidance and help. The best job you seek may not be entirely what you envisioned. Best does not equate with richness (as in money). Abundance takes many forms and it takes a person who is rich in spirit to recognize this.

The best job will not bring you happiness if you don't know the true concept of happiness. If you look for something outside of yourself, such as a job, to make your reality, you will be disappointed. For only when you are happy with who you are, the best job will remain ever elusive. Believe in yourself, believe you deserve the best, and the best you shall have. (Shamani)

Can we succeed working in a non-traditional job?

If you believe in and love what you are doing, you will succeed. How do you define a traditional job versus a non-traditional job? Is a traditional job what most people value or is their life what they value? If you can answer this question as it applies to you, then you will know if you can succeed in a non-traditional job.

A non-traditional job requires a lot of self-discipline and self-motivation. In effect, you are the director of your life. You can choose what others have traditionally chosen for you. Sometimes, you may be confused about what direction you are going in. In order to succeed in a non-traditional job, you must first identify your ambitions, desires, and goals in life. Think of what has helped you to achieve these things in the past. If you align who you are with what you are doing, you will surely succeed.

But ultimately, can you measure the success of your life by the job you perform? Is your lifestyle dependent on your job? Can you learn to live more simply and enjoy what you have?

Can you learn to measure what you have by what you truly have instead of by what you do not have? Can you put a price on knowledge and wisdom? If you can put a price on these things, then you might be best suited to remain in or seek a traditional job.

You have the choice to succeed or not to succeed. Others may facilitate your choice and take part in your success. But only you can determine whether you have made the right choice. A non-traditional job or a traditional job, where does your success lie? I would advise you to experience both types, and then make the choice. For when you make the choice, you are more likely to succeed. Focus on what you want and it shall be yours. And when you have found success, share it with others. (Asmuth)

What role does ego play in our growth?

Ego, yours and mine, what to do about it?

Visionaries of the east, visionaries of the west—come together. Together we are one.

Visions of terror, whose is better? Yours, mine, his, hers—what does it matter? Who laid claim to it first?

Ego, the great booster in our mind. Ego tells us what is good, what feels right. Although sometimes it goes astray, wandering aimlessly without direction or purpose.

Ego can control one's life, one's whole life. If left to go astray, it can be devastating, much like a tornado, devouring everything in its path. So I say to you, be aware of it (ego) and keep it under control. The mind is ever so powerful. Without it we would wither away, but left unguarded, it can cut a path of destruction, leaving no prisoners in its wake. So I say, the same is with ego. (Asmuth)

How can we value ourselves more?

This I say to you, affairs of the heart. Trust yourself, value yourself, see merit in everything you do. Trees of the forest need nourishment or wither they will. Prominence in character, lessons await you. Perseverance is the key to this. Abstain from trials of the heart, words await to be spoken.

Truth is but a heartbeat away. Trust thyself, walk carefully, who knows what awaits you? Glorious beginnings need support. Support thyself, see value in everything you do. Chiefs' feathers are plucked from the headdress one by one to reveal the mask of insincerity. So I tell you, be sincere in all your efforts. Your efforts are for naught.

Candles glow, aspirations reached, dawn of new ideas. Value comes from truth, be true to yourself. Do it for the love of it. Many of you search a lifetime for that which makes you prominent, gold-like without any care for the self. Gold is nice to look at, but to behold is better. By better, I mean the essence of the gold, not the material aspect. Materialism takes away from the heart, leads us down a path of destruction. Pay attention to the affairs at hand—sincerity, simplicity abound.

Beach sands turn different colors when the ocean lays upon it. The sands of time beckon you to pull a feather from my cap. See it, feel it, see value in it, know it, value it, be it. Then you will know value. This is all I say to you. Gratsi. (Shamani)

Why do so many of us lack self-esteem and self-confidence? What is the actual root cause?

So many of you do not trust the universal energy. You are afraid of who you are. Your lives are based on what others think of you.

The root cause of low self-esteem and self-confidence is your inability to believe in yourself. If you believe in yourself, anything is possible. But so often, you weigh yourself down with the ideas of impossibility.

You must learn to dance like the eagle. Have you ever thought of just letting yourself go, allowing the uninhibited part of you to be freely expressed? You must find the courage to be yourself. Does it really matter what others might think or how they will judge you?

If you remain in your cocoon of security, you will always lack self-esteem and self-confidence. Once you venture out of your cocoon, you will develop a sense of who you are. Feel free to be yourself, the confidence and esteem you lack can be found in free and creative expression of the self (soul).

Believe and affirm that you have the right to free and creative expression. Cast aside the doubts and fears that keep you a prisoner to yourself. Look deep within yourself and discover who you really are. Let that part of you rise to the surface. See value in who you are. Be your own cheerleader, rally to the cause. Hoist your own sails and set yourself free. A new world filled with self-confidence and self-esteem awaits your discovery. The question is, will you sit idly listening to your doubts and fears or will you stand up for and affirm what you believe in—yourself? (Shamani)

How can we motivate ourselves internally?

See the vulture as it circles its prey. It knows what it must do to survive. If it stops circling and leaves the area for one moment, other vultures or predators may lay claim to the feast. The vulture sees a feast while remembering the famine. It once thought the famine would last forever. But forever is never, for there is always an abundance of food for those who know where to look.

So I ask you, do you know where to look for spiritual food? If you say outside of yourself, I cannot agree. Like the vulture, you know what you want. Now you must persevere, be patient, and wait for opportunities to awaken your motivational energy.

Do not wait too long, for you may miss the daylight and sleep through the night.

Many a person has asked this question before you, how can I motivate myself internally? Do the leaves resist the wind or do they allow the wind to caress them? So I ask you, do you resist your inner voice? Your inner voice can lead you on many journeys, both near and far. But are you ready to travel or are you content to stay where you are?

What is motivation, but an extension of yourself. You have all that it takes to be successful. Motivation is what takes you there. Do not be afraid of success and the benefits it brings. Why, each of you is a success—your life on earth is a testimony to that.

If you do not like something, change it, change the way you feel about it, or accept it as it is. Become motivated to treat yourself well, do not sell yourself short. You have all the energy you need and more. No one can be the director of your life, except you. You are a symbol of motivational excellence. Prepare a seat for yourself at the feast, the feast that will feed you for all eternity.

Motivation lasts for eternity. May you eternally be motivated to seek eternity. (Shamani)

Why do we use money as a measure of our security?

You clothe yourself in money like a security blanket. The blanket can be as thin or thick as you make it. Money is used by you to gauge your success. You use it as a measuring stick, by which all other things are measured. So much of your life revolves around money. Do I have money, do I have enough now, will I have enough for the future?

Money seems to be interlocked with your ego. The ego is very powerful and actually thrives on the aspect of money. What can I buy to satisfy myself?

Money is such an integral part of your society. It seems that you could not do without it. It was not always like this. Those before you traded goods for services. You know this as bartering. Now, you use paper and metal to trade for goods and services.

And you put so much value in that paper and metal. The more someone has, the better they are. What do they really have? What if that paper and metal suddenly was worthless—what would they have?

So I say to you, do not put so much value in paper, metal, or material things. When you clothe yourselves in these things, you become enslaved by them.

Live more simply and you will realize how little you really need. You will also be happier. The road to success is not paved with complexity. (Shamani)

Is there scarcity?

Do you miss what you don't have? Do you need what you don't have? The haves, the have-nots—always a source of controversy. You always have exactly what you need!

Quantity is not an issue, though it may be an issue dear to your heart. Your heart needs to pump blood. Unless you are severely injured and lose blood, you have enough blood. Your body circulates and recycles blood. There is no scarcity here.

When it comes to time, many of you see scarcity personified. I hear you say, there isn't enough time in a day. The reason there isn't enough time is because your mind deals in finite terms. Minutes, hours, days, months, years—a measure of what is "possible" or "impossible." Time is a creation of your mind. Ever notice that some days, time seems to speed up or slow down. Could it be your mind is speeding up or slowing down?

Nothing is scarce unless you make it scarce or think it is scarce! As I've said before, you will always have everything you need and not necessarily everything you want. If you had a million dollars, would you really need it? No, you could only buy the things you want. Your needs would cost far less.

You may say to yourself, there isn't enough love in the world. But I say, there's enough love in each one of you to blanket the whole world. If you open yourself, there can be no scarcity.

If you put limits on your mind, you will always feel there isn't enough. (Asmuth)

How do we let go of our need for excess material possessions?

First, you must acknowledge that you have excess material possessions. Next you must ask yourself, why do you feel the need to acquire so many material possessions! Are the material possessions a substitute for the absence of love in your life? Do the material possessions give you a sense of security?

Material possessions are often symbols of false love and security. They often fulfill a temporary need in you. I ask you—what if you were stripped of all your material possessions? What would you have? The answer is you would have your mind, body, and spirit. This is what you have when you enter and depart the earth plane. When you enter the earth plane, you are in your mother's womb. You feel a sense of love and security. Then you go through your life trying to find love and security through the acquisition of material things. Love and security can only be truly found by going within yourself. You are the gatekeeper, you have the key to love and security.

I ask you to look within yourself and see value in who you are. You are a spirit filled with love. Learn to see value in everything. Once you see the value, you will see no need to possess anything. Remember that you can use something without possessing it by recognizing its value. (Asmuth)

How can we attain great wealth?

You can attain great wealth by standing on your principles. In order to be successful at anything, you must build a foundation. The foundation must be strong and solid enough to withstand the greatest force.

For some, great wealth is seemingly measured in dollars. If you build an empire based on money, when there is no value to money, where will you be? I see that money buys you things that seemingly bring happiness into your life. What value do these things have?

You can't buy spirit nor can you put a dollar value on it. You can buy false power and love but when all is said and done, what do you have? Remember, you are what you become.

As I said before, you must build a foundation to attain great wealth. The foundation of "you" is your soul. Indeed, you have great wealth right now, you have an abundance of everything you need. If you are traveling the path of truth, love, and light, you have great wealth. Do you not recognize what you have?

Your mind is an unlimited treasure-trove of information. Much of your brain lies dormant like the ancient treasures. So many of you are trying to find treasures outside of yourself, ways to make you wealthy monetarily. You spend your days and most of your life trying to make money. You somehow think that once you have a lot of money, all your problems will be magically solved. Life will be better, no worries, ah—the easy life.

Until you are rich in spirit, you will continue to search for other things to make you wealthy.

Beauty, love, truth, and light are priceless, but all who choose to embrace them can. (Asmuth)

How can we bring abundance into our lives?

Let your spirit be your guide. Know that all of what your soul needs is abundant in the world. In order to bring abundance into your life, you must first open yourself. The purple robes are here for those who will wear them. You must tell yourself that you are worthy of and deserve abundance.

Abundance takes many forms, it is often disguised with or a part of something else. As an example, treasures are often buried beneath the ground. In order to find the treasure, you must first believe that it exists. Then you must use a map to find it. If no map exists, then you must trust your intuitive ability to lead you to the treasure. The measures you have taken to develop your intuitive ability will be instrumental in your locating the treasure. So, not only do you have to believe the treasure exists, you also have to believe in yourself.

So I say it is the same with abundance, believe it exists and believe that you can attract it to yourself. Focus on that which you need and ask your spirit guides, guardian angels, or those who watch over you to assist you with attracting abundance to your life. Ask that the abundance you need be provided, in accordance with your true higher purpose. When you have received abundance, thank yourself and your spirit guides, guardian angels, or those who watch over you.

May the abundance you receive be used in the spirit of love. Always share what you have. Share the gift of love and it shall come back to you. (Asmuth)

How can we evolve into a happier, more fulfilled, individual state? Collectively?

Happiness is a state of consciousness. Happiness takes many forms and can be expressed both individually and collectively. In order to evolve into a happier, more fulfilled, individual state, you must elevate yourself to a higher level of consciousness.

When the spirit is free and unrestricted, then you are happy. Examine in yourself what makes you feel free. Allow yourself to feel free and happy.

When your spirit is weighed down, you lack a sense of freedom. Do not allow yourself to become bogged down with concerns and issues that are not dear to your heart. If you are doing something you do not like, you are denying your spirit freedom. Are you really happy where you are? You can deny yourself the feelings of happiness, but who do you really hurt? You can continue to mask your unhappiness through routine and rehearsed behavior.

Material possessions do not bring you happiness, they are only distractions. Material possessions only weigh your spirit down. You find ways to escape yourself, you are truly afraid of happiness.

For those of you who are aware that you can evolve into a happier, more fulfilled, individual state, allow your spirit to soar like the eagle. Visualize yourself in a cocoon of happiness. You are surrounded with love. Do not feel restricted by the cocoon because you have the freedom to expand the size of the cocoon. As the cocoon becomes larger, so does the happiness that surrounds you.

As you evolve into a happier, more fulfilled, individual state, you will find that others (people, plants, animals, insects, rocks, and all other things in the universe) will be attracted to you. You will be like a magnet of happiness, many will be attracted to you. I ask you to share your happiness.

When the collective consciousness of all souls on earth achieves a state of happiness, all who stand in the light will see the truth. The truth is that you have the right to eternal happiness. (Shamani)

How will we know if we are doing our life's work?

Do you believe in yourself? Do you believe what you are doing is your life's work? You alone hold the key to success. Make wise decisions and choices, and the fruits shall follow. Spiritual abundance is paramount to your life's work. I am here to guide you along the way. White robes which I wear represent pure beauty and love. Clothe yourself and stand firm in what you believe.

Life paths are always chosen with a true purpose in mind. If you await a sign, go to where the tree is chopped down. See the purpose, the beauty of the tree, the obvious neglect of those who took a life. Indifference, intolerance reigns in your world. But to this end I tell you, you have the tools, the tools of wisdom and conscious thought. Respect all life. Envision a new tomorrow.

To all who wear the robes of insecurity, I ask you—is it not better to try than to never have tried at all? Cast your wishes out and see them return to you. All I ask is that the truth be known. You are the vehicle by which I live.

This is all I have to say for now. (Asmuth)

Chapter 8:
Answers About Life Stages

From a seed of love you were born, conceived in the light of the spirit. A spiritual being composed of a body, mind, and soul. Now you find yourself in a place you know little about. You seem confused about your place in life, there has to be more to it than this, you say. Indeed there is, but you need look no farther than yourself. This is your life and believe it or not, you have chosen it.

Life stages, each one carrying a thousand wishes. But which wishes will be granted and at what stage of life? In order to answer this, you must first read the questions and answers in this chapter. For until you have read what has already been written, you will lack the precise knowledge and wisdom necessary to make your journey.

From childhood to adolescence, to young adulthood, to adulthood, and finally to old age, many of you advance in age without knowing why. Life stages—are these random events in themselves or are these part of a well-devised plan? Think about this, if you had all the knowledge and wisdom as a child, would you truly know how to use it properly? Life is a progression toward the truth, the truth is what you (your soul) seeks.

The truth can be discovered in any stage of your life. When you are ready to receive the truth, you shall open yourself to receive it. For some, this may occur in childhood. For others, the truth may be a product of old age. The important thing is to be aware that the truth exists.

Your life stages are filled with many challenges and lessons. Until you have learned how to master each life stage, you will seem presumed to repeat that stage over and over again. How many of you are still living in your childhood? Are the memories of the past so glorious that you can't bear the thought of living in the present?

All I ask of you is to take each stage in life one step at a time. There should be no rush to get to the end, for in the end, you shall enter another stage of life, a new beginning. The question is, will you be ready? (Shamani)

Why are we born only to eventually die?

Birth is a cycle. Death is a cycle. Together the two cycles make up the cycle of life. Think of the birth of ideas. An idea starts as a glimmer of light. As the idea becomes stronger, it is able to stand on its own. In turn, other ideas are born from this one idea. Soon that one idea shines brilliantly for all to see. But the idea of one cannot brilliantly shine forever. It becomes weary from the intense scrutiny placed upon it. So it withers away and "dies" in a sense, but is never forgotten. For the ideas born from it (one) are a lasting tribute. And so you see, the same is with each of you.

Think of yourselves as an idea. In birth, you are given all the tools to attain knowledge and wisdom in this lifetime. Once you have attained a certain level of knowledge and wisdom, you must pass the tools on to others. Do not see death as the end-all to life, it is only the beginning of a new set of challenges. Your spirit (soul) is always alive, it is only your perception of life and your physical body that seemingly "dies."

Find the courage and strength to live each day as if it were your first day on the earth plane. Do not limit your thinking to what you are restricted by. Venture out into the uncharted wilderness of your mind, body, and spirit. You may find many surprises along the way. Do not be alarmed for you can change what does not fit.

You have the freedom to live or die. Do not see this as a choice, for in death you are renewed by life, and in life you are renewed by death. You may be confused by what I say, but be assured that life and death are one in the same.

I caution you not to take your own life prematurely for surely you will find death. Allow yourself to be continuously reborn into the concepts or ideas of love and truth. These two concepts will help you to make the transition between birth and death, as well as death and birth.

Remember, birth and death are not as important as the way in which you choose to live. (Asmuth)

What do we learn from childhood?

Childhood, an age of innocence. You learn that everything around you is filled with beauty. You see things as they truly are without any superficial painted images. I speak of the early stage of childhood.

The leaves are green as they appear. You do not see color differences in people. There is no black, white, yellow, or red to differentiate between. The child only sees the soul of another person. Only until the child is subjected to various images of what is "right" and "wrong" by the elders is the child's perception changed.

Childhood prepares you for the rest of your life. What you learn at this stage will propel you into adulthood. If you have not learned your lessons as a child, you will learn them as an adult. Some lessons are easy, some are hard. If you make choices easily, your lessons won't be difficult. However, if you resist imminent change, your lessons will be difficult.

As a child, you are given a vision of all that can be. You are given all the tools you need to create your own vision. A vision of the future, build something that will last. What you create should be a reflection of yourself.

As an adult, you should be a symbol for all the children to follow. Share your positive experiences and transform them into lessons of learning. For the children represent the future. Let life on earth be without end. (Shamani)

What do we learn from adolescence?

Adolescence is a gift, a gift passed down through the ages. It is a bridge between childhood and adulthood. Often a difficult time for many, some never make it through.

Life is full of phases, like the phases of the moon. All contribute to the fullness of the moon. Although only part of the moon is light, in time the moon will be fully lit. So it is, I say, the same with you.

During adolescence, an abundance of ideas and choices open themselves. Feelings are enhanced, the mystical fantasies of childhood become real. Reality is at your doorstep, but all the tools you require are not provided to you.

You start to realize you have choices. But you also realize there is a certain amount of responsibility that accompanies these choices. Your choices have long-lasting consequences.

Adolescence can be a joyful time or a painful time or a mix of both. It is certainly a time of growth, both mentally and spiritually. Emotions run high, too. The answers are out there and you seem ready to conquer them. Few can tell you what the answers are, for you feel you have them.

So I say to you who are adolescents, sit back, take notice, and listen. Build your bridge from childhood to adulthood on a solid foundation. For if you rush through the process, the bridge will surely collapse. What you do now dictates the rest of your life. A solid bridge will make the transition easier and you can travel back and forth easier. (Asmuth)

What do we learn from young adulthood (20s–30s)?

The crow flies west instead of south for the winter. It is a symbol for you to follow. What you learn from young adulthood is how to trust your intuitive thoughts and feelings. You learn to develop your own character based on what you have learned in the past twenty-plus years.

In your childhood, you build a foundation of thoughts, feelings, and ideas. You develop a sense of who you are. As you develop from a child to a young adult, you cross a path which leads you down some very challenging roads.

Your life is similar to a tree branch. There is the main body of the branch which symbolizes who you are and what you stand for. But there are also several offshoots from the branch. These offshoots symbolize the desires you have to go beyond yourself. If these desires are strong enough, a new branch will take shape. Think of springtime when a tree bears new buds. The new buds symbolize new thoughts, feelings, and ideas. In a sense, you feel renewed in the spring, just like the tree. So I say to you, branch out from yourself and discover who you are.

Young adulthood can be the most important growth period of your life on the earth plane. It is a time to develop your strengths and weaknesses, both of these make you stronger. Strength cannot be entirely measured by physical means. Strength is measured in terms of the emotional, mental, spiritual, and physical states of being. It is equally important to develop your mind, body, and spirit.

Remember that young adulthood is very important. For in this stage of your life, you will grow and learn at a rapid rate. The doors to rapid growth are open to you. Will you open or close the doors? It is up to you. Will you fly south for the winter because everyone tells you this is the way, or will you fly west because your intuition tells you so? Trust your intuitive ability and soon you will find the path to the light and truth. (Shamani)

What can we learn from middle age (40s, 50s)?

The conceptions of a few are an intrusion into the minds of many. Do not let others dictate your stages of life. Your concept of age is based on a device devoted to time. Do not devote yourself to the ideas of many. Instead embrace your independence, for now is the time to beat your own drum.

What does middle age connote? What are you in the middle of? You only set a limit on yourself and what you can accomplish. Accomplishments can not be measured in a time sequence. Your life can be expanded from the point of your soul's conception. Life is without end.

"Middle age" can serve as an accelerator or a decelerator, depending on how you perceive it. The same can be said for the young and the elders. Wisdom can be attained at any point in your life on earth and beyond. The limits you set on yourself will keep you a slave to yourself. Your life is like a puzzle. You may have all the pieces to solve it but do you know how all the pieces fit together?

For those who are stuck in between "childhood" and "old age," I ask you to take what you have learned as a child, both the wisdom and free spirit, and launch yourself into a new era of thinking and feeling. Take time to look around you, there is much you have overlooked. The missing pieces of the puzzle are scattered around. But you can find them, if you use the wisdom you have been given.

As you reflect on your past, look at your reflection in the mirror. Are you happy—are you sad? Do you wish you had lived differently? All of this is in the past—what you do right here and now is what will make a difference. Do not dwell in the past, recover from your childhood—life awaits you. You can either take the escalator or elevator to the top floor. But remember, what do you see in an elevator? You remain in a box with other people and get nowhere fast.

Spend time with your children and parents. For those whose children and/or parents have passed on, I share your need for solitude. To you, I give a bouquet of golden roses. May you never forget that those who have passed over are comforted and loved. May you also find comfort and love in knowing this.

"Middle age" is a time of reflection. Let it be a reflection of who you really are. Stand tall and be honest with yourself. Take off the disguises which mask your true identity. By doing these things, you will truly discover that which is timeless—your life. (Shamani)

What do we learn from old age?

Old age, timeless wonder, do you tire from the long journey? But has it not been worth it, think of all the wisdom and knowledge you have gained.

Those who are old wish they were younger, those who are young wish they were older. Seems a shame to waste the youth on the young and the old age on the elderly. Seems like there should be a role reversal. There are some who voice this, but many embrace youth and old age.

Old age is an accumulation of thoughts, ideas, feelings, and lessons. It seems once you've learned it (the meaning of life), it is time for you to pass over.

The term you use, "old age," is somewhat confusing. For we all have had many lives, how "old" are we really? But in this life, many seem older than they are. Wisdom comes to those who embrace it.

Our life journeys are filled with lessons. We choose the lessons and the pace at which we learn.

Age is timeless, only a gauge by which you measure your life on Earth. What you do with your life determines the age to which you live. (Asmuth)

What role do our elders play in our lives and in society?

The elders are the keepers of the wisdom. If you look to your elders for the answers you seek, you will see that only years of trial and error have made them so wise. You too will one day become an elder. Wisdom and knowledge are to be shared. You can have all the knowledge and wisdom in the universe and still have no knowledge and wisdom how to use it.

Protect the elders of your society. If you cast them out or shut them in, you do a great disservice to yourself as well as them. Their needs and your needs are equally important. You may not think of your elders as contributing much to your life, but I say you are blind to the past. If you could only walk the thousands of miles they have walked, you would see that they have contributed so much to your life.

The elders have much to teach you, if you only open your mind and soul. They can teach you things that no history book can teach you. For they have feelings, thoughts, and ideas that tell a different story. The story is in their own words, neither fact nor fiction. The words of life emanate from their lips. The words they speak are expressions of freedom. Freedom from guilt and despair. They have seen and done it all, their life is a testimony to that.

So I ask you to respect and revere your elders. Hold them in high regard. The elders who are wise know what I speak of. The person who is wise does not claim to be wise, for wisdom cannot be clouded with ego. Let the wise elders teach you the way to freedom, freedom from the addictions that hold you a prisoner to yourself. Set yourself free so that you may open yourself to the knowledge and wisdom.

Remember that the elders will teach you what you will one day know. You can learn it now or later, it is possible to see the future in the present moment. Do you know what I say now or will you say what I know later? (Shamani)

How should we treat our elders?

The eagle rises after a long night's sleep. Once thought dead, he has risen again to embrace the new day. A new day is dawning, the whole world awaits your arrival. Will you embrace the new day or will you let it pass without notice? And so I say to many of you, treat your elders with respect, treat each other with respect. You can learn so much from one another. Do not restrict yourself to your circle of life. Expand your circle to include others. The circle grows with love. Love is the eternal blessing bestowed upon you.

The wolf cries in pain. Will you try to heal the wolf or will you walk away in fear? The wolf has provided much of your needs, it has walked a thousand miles ahead of you. Do you realize this? Think of what I say in terms of the elders, those who have walked the earth before you. They were once bound by chains (their own ideas). But they found the key to unlock the chains. Now you walk effortlessly, for those before you have marked the trail.

The elders do not ask to be glorified, only to be recognized. They are aware of who you are and where you have been—it is no secret. The secret to happiness is to live a "long" life in a way which you can be proud of. "Long" is relative, I do not speak of time. I speak of "long" in terms of stretching your abilities, being all that you are.

Many of you may think that you know more than your elders. Indeed, you may, but does that make you a better person? If you know more, then teach others what you know. Soon, you will be an elder of knowledge. Soon, the elders will come to you seeking knowledge and wisdom. See how they treat you and reply the same.

Old age is not a curse but a blessing. You can always relive memories but you must live today to make a memory for tomorrow. Remember who you are and where you've come from. For one day, others will see you as an elder and treat you as you have treated the elders today. I leave you with three simple words to help you: respect, love, and understanding. Treat your elders accordingly. (Shamani)

What can we learn from our grandchildren?

Your grandchildren are a symbol of life never-ending. Think about what you are leaving them in terms of wisdom and understanding. Grandchildren look up to their grandparents with awe. It almost seems as if the grandparents hold the crystal ball containing all the wisdom of the world.

From your grandchildren, you can learn the value of youth. When we are young, we don't see the true gift we behold. The whole world is in our hands, we can mold it the way we want (if only in our minds), the spirit of adventure is prevalent, and yet we don't "see" it. We want to grow older. It is only after we grow older (beyond childhood) that we try to recapture that spirit.

You can learn to enjoy every moment of your lives. Do not be envious of the young or old. There is beauty and wisdom in being both. Find comfort and peace where you are, right here, right now. The present is all that matters. For if you are not content with yourself now, what makes you think the future will be any different? (Asmuth)

Why do some people move often while others remain at their birthplace?

Each soul has a different destiny. Destiny is your individual choice, both here and beyond. We are all free spirits. Some spirits are restless while others find stability in the moment.

You are the director of your life, you have two eyes to see with. You have a vision of what your life will be. You are on a personal voyage of discovery. You may visit many places, for you there is a spirit of adventure. Different people and different cultures pique your interest. For you, life is not about staying in one place too long. There are personal challenges and mysteries that await your discovery. You wish to discover the true secrets of yourself. The universe is in constant motion, why shouldn't you be. For you, life can not be summized in one experience. You are on an eternal vision quest. I say this to those who move often. Let your spirit soar and take you to the far reaches of your mind.

To those who remain at their birthplace, I say that you move with great purpose and intent. You have a vision of your life, you hold and embody that vision. You find stability in one place, the world does not entirely pique your interest. The excitement you desire can be found in one place. Yet within one place, there are many challenges and lessons for you. You are the captain of a thousand ships. The ships always stay in port awaiting your orders to sail. The seas seem rough and uncharted. We shall wait another day before we sail, you say. There is much to do here on land anyway. For you, it is better to remain at your birthplace than to sail uncharted waters. The security and stability of the "home" is what you seek. Let others who are willing to make the journey cast off.

Mobility and stability allow each soul to discover their true potential. Every soul takes a different journey but alas every soul converges into one. Let your spirit soar and discover who you are. Above all, follow your own vision! (Shamani)

What do you think about divorce?

Marriage is an institution. Divorce is an institution. Are these two institutions based entirely on love? Too often, I see many of you entering into marriage or divorce out of convenience. You disregard the institutions that you have created and supported.

If you marry, it should be for the sole reason of love, not for money, convenience, or because it's what everyone expects of you. Whose life is it, yours or theirs? Most often, when you are not in love, the marriage can only deteriorate into divorce.

What is divorce but a separation? Why did you get married in the first place? In a sense, marriage is an escape for many of you. When you can not face yourself, you attempt to escape into a world of fantasy which often climaxes in marriage.

In order for the institution of marriage to work, you must commit to loving yourself. For if you do not love yourself, do you think marriage will change this? There are many ways for a couple to express love for each other. Find the ways that keep you together or separate you. Divorce is neither "right" nor "wrong," it is what you choose to make it.

If you are not happy with your marriage, do not amuse yourself by being miserable in it. Either change or accept it. You are the key to your happiness. Marriage and divorce are institutions of control and ownership. You can commit to loving yourself and another person, or loving an institution for the rest of your life. If you choose to live by institutions, then surely you will die by them also. (Shamani)

How can we help our children deal with divorce?

Innocent pawns in a game of chess. Not only must you help your children but also your inner child. Isn't that—the inner child—who led you down this path. In order to help your children, you must look at the situation through the eyes of a child. What do you see? Pain, confusion, separation, anxiety, frustration, anger, only to name a few!

Think of the difficulty you have in dealing with divorce. Then project an increased level of difficulty and you will see what your child is experiencing. Experience is the best teacher but it can also be the most difficult. I cannot give you a specific answer for each child. You know your child and his or her emotional and mental needs. Try to nurture those needs by communicating open love for them. Hug them and tell them that they are not to blame for the divorce.

It is often very difficult for a child to accept that mommy and daddy don't want to be with them anymore. All of what they have grown to know is suddenly turned upside-down and no one is there to tell them it will be all right. They will question whether this is a dream or reality, or both?

Talk to your children, let them know how you feel. Then answer any questions they may have as best you can. I ask you not to defame your spouse. It might be better for you and your spouse to collectively talk to your child. You may even find that you can reconcile your differences. Children are often the best mediators, if you value their knowledge and wisdom.

If you can not reconcile your differences, then seek to part from each other in an aura filled with love. Accept each other for what each of you is. See that you both have grown in different directions and have decided to change your life for the better. May your divorce be forever surrounded in the spirit of love and peace. And may your children be a part of your lives forever. (Shamani)

How can we help ourselves deal with divorce?

The eagle stands alone, waiting for an answer. Can the answer to this question be etched in stone? I think not, for each of you is different. What is divorce based on but differences of opinions, lifestyle, and love.

Divorce is essentially a division of yourself from another person. The differences that brought you together are now the differences that set you apart. Do not fear what is to be. It is better that both of you have realized that the life you dreamed of is no more. Who can put a number on love? Can you find a book or source that will tell you how long you will be married or in love? Not even a crystal ball can tell you with any accuracy.

Fate or destiny, you seem to be ruled by it. But then you have chosen this path, so you indeed rule it. Do not seek to blame the other person for what you did not share. Just thank yourself for making a responsible choice to leave your marriage behind. It is time for you to move on, you are on a path of self-discovery in which you are the guide.

If children and/or assets were a product of the marriage, you must take care in preserving both. Your children are the most important, do not treat them as things which can be divided down the middle. Think of your life being torn in half and you are given two pieces which do not fit anymore. How would you feel? It is important that you talk to your children and help them understand how you feel. This will help them to make the transition.

Before I go further, I ask you to take one step backward to before you got married. Ask yourself: what did I want? what did I feel? and who was I? Do you feel the same way now? Are you asking yourself the same questions? How will your life be different from now on? Seek to better yourself by getting in touch with your emotions.

Divorce brings a sense of finality. You can choose to grow or stagnate. Whatever you do, do it out of love. One day you will be whole again, possibly married again. Do not carry the misfortune of one marriage to another. Seek to find what is missing in your life and grow into that void. Surround yourself with love.

Remember the eagle (you) shall return to the nest and stand alone once again. In your aloneness, you will see that there are others like you who have traveled the same road. For them, the answers did not always come easy but they did find the answers.

And you shall find the answers that you seek. Open yourself (your mind, body, and spirit) and you shall receive them. (Shamani)

How can people come to terms with their conception of death?

Death, a bridge across forever. You see it every day. Yes, you have survived another day. Death, a measure of where we have been and where we are going. Going to hell or going to heaven is what so many ask.

Death is a resting-place. It is not something to fear. With death comes rebirth. You have experienced this throughout your life.

That moment between death and life can be very scary. You are alone much like when you were born. It is in this moment that you are faced with the eternal question—where am I?

Death is what you make of it. It can be enjoyable or painful. Death is a test of faith, do you believe in yourself? Who am I?

Conceived in the light, so shall you return to the light. Many souls await you, your beliefs await you. The final script of your life has been written. Will there be a sequel? Only you can decide.

What lies beyond may not be as glorious as what you left here on Earth. The way you live your life will determine your "afterlife." I say this not in a punishing way at all. You will find that forgiveness comes to all who seek it.

In death, you shall see truth. (Shamani)

What would you say to those who are grieving for their loved ones?

Light, essence, angels of purity watch over you. The stars above do not shine without you. There is a higher purpose, although not visible to you now. Perpetual motion, souls reunited with loved ones. Although you grieve now, it is with my deepest love I say to you do not worry. For you too, one day, shall be reunited with those who strain your heart.

The fiddler plays a violin, sweet sounds. A mist lowers over the valley, covering everything, till the sun bursts forth in a new day.

Love does not perish, those you grieve for hear you. They hear your wants, your wishes, but they too are safe.

Eruptions of the heart, glorified, welcome them for soon you too shall be with them. Do not curse the ground you walk on. Senseless tragedy or divine purpose—you be the judge. But who do you judge—those before you?

Keep a silent vigil in your soul. Open your heart and let the bountiful love and truth flow in. Let it flow like a waterfall and soon you shall be refreshed.

The light shines down upon you to give you renewal of spirit. Love abounds, love is plentiful, know that love will keep you strong. Go forth into the light and seek the eternal truth, the truth awaits you. A tunnel of love, you are embraced by it. See it, feel it, know it—know that love is real.

In death, we only come to see kindred spirits. Spirits of love, peace, and harmony. A symphony of souls bonding through love. Love without blame, desire, denial. Love in the truest sense. Be comforted by what I say. You are loved so dearly. (Asmuth)

What is the best way to spend our lives?

There are many ways to spend your lives, but can I say what is best for each of you? You are the ruler of your destiny. Can anyone else say what the best way is to spend your life? Many may try to tell you what is best for them, but is it best for you?

Strength and courage walk hand in hand. You have both the strength and courage to decide what is best for you. You may not always like the consequences of your choices. But remember, you make the best choices possible, given all you know. Use the knowledge and wisdom you have developed, for your life depends on it.

If you spend your life seeking the truth and sharing the knowledge and wisdom you have acquired, you will have found the best way to spend your life. Be a symbol of free and creative expression. The best way to spend your life is to be truly who you are. Honor and respect your own life path and the paths of others.

In order to be truly who you are, you must identify one thing about yourself that truly makes you happy. Once you've found that one thing, which can only be love, build a monument to it. Then spend the rest of your life sharing love and being happy.

Some of you may know a better way to spend your life, but I ask you, are you being true to yourself? Best does not equate with truth, for truth can only be what is best for you. (Asmuth)

Chapter 9:
Answers About Who We Are

Who am I, a question asked by many for thousands of years. Sometimes we can get so wrapped up in ourselves that we shut out everyone else. Whose world is this? The world I speak of is the earth plane, designed for your immediate gratification and pleasure. What a concept and all you have to do is share it with others. But as difficult as it seems, it's easy. Do not the trees stand side by side with the rocks in the forest? They love and respect each other and they realize and understand without one, the other can not survive. And you thought that trees and rocks were lifeless. I am here to tell you just the opposite.

So, opposites attract and that is why so many of you have been brought together on one plane of existence. Think of your life on Earth as a model for other civilizations beyond the Earth. Many of us (your guardian angels, spirit guides, and those who watch over you) await the predicted outcome. So it is up to each and every one of you to bring out the best in yourself. Apply positive thoughts and feelings to every aspect of your life.

You have many questions about why there are so many different people, races, and cultures. The differences are only those you see on the surface. Look deeper into the mind and soul of everything. Every one of you, for the most part, has the same body organs, the same heartbeat. Yet, what you see physically in each other determines the differences that distance you from each other.

So I ask you, as you read the questions and answers in this chapter, ask yourself, how is my soul similar to every other soul on the planet Earth? Who are we but a reflection of ourselves. Knowledge and wisdom comes to those who read, so I invite you to join with me in recording a new history for the Earth by reading what already has been written. (Shamani)

Why are communities seemingly falling apart?

Apart the threads of sanity or insanity are tested. The strain of the family growing apart. Strike down each other with words or thoughts, it's just the same. A lack of order, a lack of respect for your brethren. Treat them as sovereign—how can you cast a stone against your brethren without that stone returning to you?

Sow your seeds with love, work together. Help a friend, do a good deed, join hands, cry together, tell (share) a story. Be mindful of what ails you. The past cannot be changed but the whole future awaits you. Flowers need water to grow, so too, communities need people to care for people. Shut out your neighbor and you shut yourself out. (Shamani)

Why do we have so many races, cultures, and levels of existence (for example, poverty, wealth, subsistence)?

The universe is diverse, made up of a multitude of colors, shapes, sizes, and images. Beneath the images you see, all things share a common origin. You are all the same in the light.

The differences you see are in your own mind. Why are such dividing lines created? The boundaries are unreal, you are together on the earth plane to help each other. Together we (earth plane and other planes) work together for the higher good.

Many see only the faces instead of the soul.

There is enough abundance for everyone, there is no need for poverty or excessive wealth. Poverty and wealth are extremes. But I say those who are rich with money are weak in spirit. It is often better to be poor with money and be rich in spirit. Those rich in money and spirit should share with each other. Do not value one more than the other.

Remember, from one we were born, to one we shall return. Divide the lines between race and culture, and wealth and poverty, and you divide yourself. (Shamani)

What is the reason for different sexual and/or gender identities? Why is one sex valued over the other in so many cultures?

Identity is a perception of the self. Your thoughts, desires, and feelings are transformed into action. Your actions determine your identity. Ask yourself—why do I see the color red as red? The reason is it is your perception of the color, red.

Actions often speak louder than words. Your actions should be truly indicative of who you are.

The role of sex and gender in your society is based on both individual and global perceptions of the self. There are many people who are not comfortable with their assigned role, be it male or female. Just because their body parts label them male, their mind or spirit may be female. Distinctions between male and female are often a cause for controversy in your global society. Men and women who cross the lines of established sexual patterns are often labeled and cast out. They are cast out, out of fear. I speak of the label you use, "homosexual." Labels only serve to separate you as a whole. You divide your souls in doing so. The differences among all of you should be celebrated.

Male and female, homosexual and heterosexual, brother and sister, father and mother, black and white, purple and gold—the differences you see are all in your perceptions of the surface. Beneath each of these labels, there lies a spirit (soul). Each of the spirits (souls), you and I, we are all connected. (Asmuth)

Why is one sex valued over the other in so many cultures?

Cultural differences and perceptions dictate this. Either male or female is revered or denied. The root of this lies in gender bias. Squelch the female and the male shall rise, and vice versa. There is false power illuminated in this idea. These ideas are of the past, many before you have practiced them. Women revered as gods, men revered as gods.

The establishment of supremacy over the perceived weaker male or female. All of this is self-serving and destructive to all involved. But to those who resist, I commend you. It is right for you to stand up for the truth. The truth is equality for all beings, not just the chosen few. Allow your male and female energies to unite as one, and dispel all the roles and identities. Choose unity over conflict. Let the hatred be replaced with love. (Asmuth)

Why do we have different gender identities?

Gender is defined by purpose. Kings and queens square off—facing each other. The docile queen stands next to the resilient king. The jewels, the crowns, the capes could be worn by either. The colors of the capes are the same. The only difference is how the male or female fits into the cape. The jewels, capes, and crowns are similar, the purpose these things serve is to unite the king and queen. The throne is shared by both—together the king and queen are united in oneness. Without the king, the queen would surely weep in sorrow. Without the queen, the king would surely be only half. There is power in the union of male and female.

But, within each individual, whether male or female, lies the need to be characterized as an individual. Through maintaining individuality, a deeper sense of identity is manifested. The true expression of an individual spirit is paramount for growth. Different gender identities are symbolic of an individual's free expression of spirit. Expressions take many forms—I ask you to respect all forms.

Remember that each of you is composed of male and female energies. Learn to nurture these energies. Do not allow the male and female energies to create opposition within you. Instead, do as the king and queen do—square off—recognize each half as being as important as the other. Develop your own gender identity and allow the free expression of your spirit. (Asmuth)

Why do we have different races?

The golden feather I show you is the answer to your question. See the feather, it is so light and beautiful. If it were not lined with gold, would it still give the bird flight? Would the bird still radiate beauty in flight? Of course it would. And so the same is with each of you, no matter what race you have been placed (categorized) in. Your ancestors before you may have created different races, but each of you perpetuates the labels. Why? You are all souls of the universe. We are all one.

The different races you see are your own creation and perception. If you were all blind, would you still see color in each other? If you could only see the soul of another person, would the thought of race enter your mind? I ask you to see with the two eyes and the third eye you have been given. Given that you perceive different races, recognize and understand that we are all one "race." Celebrate the differences each of us shares. Respect your life and the life of every creation of the universe. Remember that love knows no distinction between color or race. When you truly love someone or something, then you see no differences between you.

On a soul level, the reason you have different races is so that you can understand that there are no differences between each of you. In your past lives, you have been a multitude of "races." If you oppress another race, then you oppress yourself. The cycle of love can continue or diminish, the choice is yours. I ask you to envision a universe devoid of race and filled with love, love for each other. Remember we are truly one. (Shamani)

Why do we have different languages?

Language is the art of communication. Each one of you speaks in a different voice or tone. No two voices are the same. Each person speaks their own language. It seems that every person expresses their identity in their own way. However, people are grouped according to certain languages.

Since the beginning, many felt the need to be different, to distinguish oneself from another. It is to the point today with billions of people on earth living in so many divisions (countries) that there are so many different languages.

Communication in the form of language takes a form which a majority of people can understand. Communication can take many forms: written, verbal, telepathic, energy, touch, and thought.

Language is as diverse as the universe itself. Language unifies people. Although many languages are spoken on earth, which may seemingly separate people, the universal language of love is spoken by everybody. (Asmuth)

Has there always been patriarchy?

Fathers of wisdom, mothers of wisdom, which does your society value more? Patriarchy is an age-old artifact, no one truly wants to admit that patriarchy has been woven into many civilizations over the years. But it is true, it has. There have been times in Earth's history, for as long as human beings have inhabited the earth, wherein masters of manipulation have placed the concept of patriarchy as the backbone of society. Who can judge if patriarchy is right or wrong? Equally, there have been times in Earth's history where matriarchy stood at the forefront of ancient wisdom.

What is wisdom based on but seeing two sides to all feelings, thoughts, and ideas.

The concept of patriarchy tends to create lines of division between all people. Just as the concept of matriarchy would do the same. If you could all learn to love and respect each other's roles and gender preferences in society, you might find that there is no need for patriarchy or matriarchy. Control and manipulation in a patriarchal sense delude the lives of many. Can you see this? The lines of division are glaring between males and females. Who wins? Who loses?

You might look to yourself and ask, what is my gender role and how am I fulfilling it? Do I see others as inferior beings or am I secure with my own identity? Who you choose to be is a direct reflection of who you are. I would hope that someday soon, the mothers and fathers of wisdom shall come together and denounce the matriarchy and patriarchy that currently dominates your societies. Take the best of both concepts and come together and unite as one in spirit. Create a spirit of love that will last forever. (Shamani)

Why are men and women, and boys and girls, raised so differently?

Why are oil drilling rigs built differently? I say because each has a different function, the strata of the earth are different from area to area. Why are different animals raised differently? Why are big ships built as opposed to small boats? These are questions which I prompt you to answer.

Men and women, boys and girls, are alike physically, mentally, and spiritually. We are all male and female in essence. Society draws distinctions based on color, physique, IQ, and other characteristics. It is what you choose.

There is a distinct difference between men and women in their respective reproductive capabilities. Through this, I see why men and women are raised differently. Aside from this, there are only slight differences.

You make the differences visible, and out of that evolves your course of action. When you make distinctions and create differences, you create more complexity for yourselves. (Shamani)

Do we incarnate into all races and cultures at some point?

Mountains of integrity are called into question. But whose integrity is questioned? Are not all races and cultures begotten from one? As I have told you, we are all one. Remember, if you strip away the physical body, you will "see" the soul. The soul is colorless and tasteless as you might have imagined. It is filled with love and true love knows no cultural or racial boundaries.

But in terms of your question, I feel I need to provide an answer which satisfies your curiosity for knowledge. In truth, you incarnate into a physical form which is most conducive to your learning. If you need to learn about racism, you might incarnate into a member of an oppressed group or an oppressor. You can view your incarnation as positive or negative. Regardless of how you view it, it is an opportunity for growth and learning.

It is important for each of you as citizens of the earth to respect the diversity of all things. Do you think that it is necessary for you to incarnate in all races and cultures? If you can learn to love yourself and others as equals, there is no need. If you can not and learn to develop hatred toward a specific race or culture, then surely you will become what you hate. So I ask you to listen to the words I speak. They are for you to hear. Mine are words of love, you may not always like what I say or how I say it. But, if you keep an open heart, you will surely receive the love I send you.

Many hearts have bled over wars of color and religion. Think of how much energy you could choose to focus on becoming one with each other. I only offer one suggestion and that is to love and respect each other's souls, regardless of racial or cultural differences. (Shamani)

Why is there racism?

Racism, shades of innocence. The innocent scorned, mocked into submission. The splatter of blood, screened across the sky. Oh dismal times! Scorn thy brother, see his fate in your hands.

Golden feathers, leaves of red—what is the difference. Your differences are your own. We all reign true in the light. The light filters through the darkness. The darkness overshadows the true purpose. Can you find fault with another without finding fault with yourself?

The truth is not colored. So why do you color your images, the images of truth? The truth reigns supreme. Your eyes are darkened, blinded by the mist. Is this a legacy to leave?

Righteous you are in your own eyes but blind to those around you. Callous thoughts, blood on my hands, I stand before you and say: Let he who casts the first stone, cast it my way.

Circles of light, saucers o'plenty, take off your disguise. The truth is spellbounding. You alone can only seek the truth. (Shamani)

What would you say to those who are racist?

The eagle stands before you, silent and bewildered, tired from the journey. The vision is clear, stand beside it, see who you are, what you've become. You who are righteous in your own eyes but blind to others. The others you scorn, you mock, are righteous too. Why do you find differences?

Red and yellow, black and white, the colors of the universe. As natural as you and I. Seek that which makes you happy—face the cursed, the wretched, the ugly. Is it you they mock and scorn?

The leaves of the forest turn green, yellow, and brown. It is all the same tree, only different shades of fantasy. Fantasy or fiction, you decide. (Shamani)

What would you say to those who are the objects of racism?

Blessed are those who stand tall. The wolf stands tall in the face of the bear. I tell you be strong and forthright. Let those who mock you, those who scorn you, step aside. The truth is marred with scars of indifference, half-truths. Stand up and be counted.

The coyote is shades of gray. Gray is a color, a mixture of black and white. Meet them halfway (your accusers). If they meet you, if they do not meet you halfway, then scorn them.

Objects of impurity, half-truths, cast out the doubt. Stand tall among the trees in the forest and be counted. The way you seek is the way of the light. Let the light penetrate the dark forest, until sunshine/sunlight bursts through. The light is the truth.

Be comforted by my words and scorn no one. Differences are only transparent, transparencies of light. (Shamani)

How can we dissolve racism?

Listen to the pigeon, it has much to tell you. I am the pigeon, oh spirited one. I never lose sight of my home, for home is where I am most comfortable. I seek to know the comfort I felt in my mother's womb. If only I could return to the darkness where I felt security. But now I stand in the light of day, pondering who

I am and what I have become. So I say to you, there is no security in the darkness. If you remain in the shadows of yourself, you will never see the light.

Racism is based on bias and prejudice, directed both at yourself and others. Racism is truly an affliction of the "heart," though it is really in your mind. Remember that the energy of your thoughts and feelings is very powerful. Power lies in the hands of the one who uses it. Remember, that which you send out (thoughts and feelings) will surely return to you. You have heard us evoke the phrase, "From one you were conceived, to one you shall return." So the same is with your thoughts and feelings. Think of this concept in terms of racism.

In order to dissolve racism, you must first dissolve your feelings of fear, doubt, anger, and hatred. Bring your soul out of the darkness. You can only find lasting comfort, love, and security in the light. All souls are equally transparent in the light. Like the pigeon, never lose sight of where you have come from—one. When you have dissolved racism in yourself, you will see that you are one (with everyone and everything) again. (Shamani)

What is the ultimate racial goal for humanity?

Black, red, yellow, or white—these are colors you as humans have created. The differences only exist in your mind.

The ultimate racial goal for humanity is unity, achieving oneness in mind, body, and spirit.

You are here on earth to help one another. No one race is better than the other. Did you not see what Adolf Hitler tried to do—create a supreme race! He failed miserably. Why did he fail? Because the idea of a supreme race was not the ultimate universal truth.

You have been given the opportunity to live in such a diverse learning environment. The differences among various people allow us to grow in our own direction. Even though you (as an individual) grow in a different direction, you (collectively) are all connected. See the diversity of people on earth as endless opportunities for learning. Each soul has sacrificed for the other, to be on this earth.

Unity can only be attained when each one of you loves, honors, and respects each other. Once unity is attained, your collective consciousness will ascend to a higher level. Until then, I ask you to be patient with one another and strive to erase the racial lines. These lines only serve to separate you from each other. (Shamani)

Why are men often valued more for the work they do than the people they are?

This is true and I see women valued more for their physical appearance than the people they are. It seems odd to me that the lines of difference between men and women are drawn so clearly.

The man sees his face in his work. It is what makes him a valuable commodity. Without work, he would not be able to see himself.

The dreams and aspirations of men are tied up in their work. Many men value their work more than they do themselves. It is often a way to escape their feelings, feelings of the heart which can't be expressed openly. Work is an outlet for the mental and physical aggressions.

You place so much emphasis on man's collective work. Men rule your cities and build your cities. They are viewed as objects.

If your work is a labor of love, then you emulate balance. You value your work and create your own self-identity. It is when your work is not your labor of love that you perceive imbalance in your life.

You can do no greater injustice to yourself than doing something you hate. You have choices, open yourself to them. Your work should be a reflection of you. (Asmuth)

Why do so many cultures deny women the development of strength and confidence?

Strength and confidence are developed from within the person, no one can deny the development of such. Can we blame others for that which we do not develop in ourselves? Let us not blame each other. I ask that you be aware of this and share it with those people who do not understand.

If you give your personal power and rights to another person willingly, you have denied yourself. I ask you to believe in yourself (those who feel they are denied the development of strength and confidence). You are a pillar of strength and confidence. Do not allow others to tell you otherwise.

Find purpose in what you do, come to know who you are. The magic lies within you. If you use the magic, you will see that you have all the strength and confidence that you need. Each of you has the magic, but few know how to use it properly.

For those of you who feel you must control others by denying the development of strength and confidence, you are only denying yourself. How can your soul be free when you hold others in contempt? If you were truly strong and confident, you would not seek to deny it in others. Strip away the coats of armor you wear. If you are strong and confident, the armor only protects you from yourself.

So I ask both sides—those who feel they are denied the development of strength and confidence, and those who feel they must deny it—to unite as one. Do not blame each other and see each other as weak. The strength and confidence you desire can not be found in the denial or control of another. Look to yourself, you are a symbol of strength and confidence. (Asmuth)

Why do so many cultures deny men free expression of emotion?

Emotion is a symbol of free expression. One of the lessons of masculine energy (collectively) is control. In energy, there exists extremes. A certain amount of masculine energy is concentrated in control. Control has focused energy with a very definite purpose.

The concept of control is exercised by many of you, both male and female. Remember that both males and females are composed of masculine and feminine energies. You often control or repress that which you do not understand. An expression of emotion is often equated with weakness of the human spirit. And so, how do you express strength? By a denial of the free expression of emotion.

But I say to all of you, male and female, when you deny yourself or others free expression of emotion, you deny yourself love. Emotion is a beautiful thing. When you deny it, your mind, body, and spirit become unbalanced. I give you an example to ponder. What if you denied men or women the right to physical exercise, to read books, to work, to obtain an education? What would you have? Surely no emotion, no feeling.

It is up to each of you to affirm your right to free expression of love. Love encompasses all your feelings, find a creative outlet for all your feelings. Do not deny yourself or anyone else the right to free expression of emotion.

To express emotion is a symbol of strength and love for yourself. Allow your emotions to flow. Love should be freely expressed and not controlled. (Asmuth)

How can we come to terms with our masculine and feminine energies, individually and collectively?

As an individual, follow what your "heart" tells you. A colonial ship captain stands on the bow of his ship, he knows who and what he is at that moment. He knows that he is doing the right thing, he is at one with himself. So I say, the same should be with you, male or female, follow the path of your heart. Your soul is like the ship. Your soul is a part of you much like the captain is a part of his ship. (Do not be frayed by my use of a man as a captain. I use the male figure only as an example.)

Be true to yourself. By this I mean, nurture both your masculine and feminine energies or feminine and masculine energies. If you suppress one, the other will come to the surface. We are all made up of feminine and masculine energies. The energies are equal and together they are one.

To see how you can come to terms with your masculine and feminine energies collectively, I give you the example of a blade of green grass. The blade of green grass grows on its own, at its own rate. However, the blade of grass grows in unison with other blades of grass. Collectively, the blades of grass are a thing of beauty. If each blade of grass had not grown on its own, the beauty of the whole would never be displayed. So it is the same with you, be who you truly are, both masculine and feminine. (Asmuth)

How can we transcend cultural barriers?

All your wishes can come true, if you believe in yourself. Place all your wishes in a bubble filled with love. Let the bubble float away and never lose sight of your wishes. They will be like whispers carried along in the wind for all to hear. Others who think like you will pick up the whispers. They in turn will place their wishes in a bubble filled with love and send it out into the universe. This cycle of love will help each of you to transcend cultural barriers.

In order for each of you to transcend cultural barriers, you must learn to cast aside your individual bias and prejudice. Can you think of a world where everyone was identical? Say for instance, everybody was just like you. What could you possibly learn about yourself? Your bias and prejudice would be turned inward all the time. Indeed, you might learn a lot about yourself, but who could you share the knowledge and wisdom with?

So now I ask you to see the differences between cultures as endless opportunities for sharing ideas and thoughts. You may find that you are enriched by interacting with other cultures. My soul speaks to your soul, though we are from different cultures. What allows me to transcend the cultural barrier is my love for you, regardless of who you are. If you wish to do the same, then let the love in your heart dissolve all barriers. You have many gifts to share with others. I ask you not to erect barriers to detour your feelings of love. Open your heart and allow your spirit of love to flow freely. (Shamani)

How can we learn to accept others without judgment?

By accepting our self. Place yourself in the light and the other in the light. Are you not equal? The more you judge, the more you resist the natural flow. If you feel the need to judge another, whether it be a human, an animal, an insect, or even a plant, walk away. Set them free, do not try to control them. They can not walk the path that you do. Do as I say is not the way to the truth.

Anger leads to judgment and where does that get us.

Why do we judge ourself? Is it out of self-love? If we loved ourself wholly, we would have no need to judge ourself or others. I am not saying this is an easy task, though it is one that requires much practice and patience. Be patient with yourself, take life at your own pace, there is no rush. Take time for yourself, sit down, read a book, share laughter with a friend.

When others do not live up to your expectations, do not judge them. Just let them go. They may tumble and fall, but that is their way. Above all, don't judge yourself, be kind to yourself and others. You'll be amazed how a kind gesture will come back to you. Give and you shall receive, judge and you will be judged. (Shamani)

How can we help restore a sense of community in our world?

Unity grows out of love. Love is the essence of life. Life is the maker of dreams. Dreams are what carry us through the day. Restore the idea of love through community, communing with one another. The communion of life, sacred as those who live it. Seek balance in your lives, do not tread on each other. Go to your neighbor, help him or her. Do not turn your back on them. Oranges can be bitter to some and sweet to others. Seek out what tastes sweet to you and find others who seek the same. (Asmuth)

Part IV:

Answers for Here and Beyond

Chapter 10:

Answers About Our Changing World

How has the world changed since you were born? Could you make a list of positive and negative changes, as you perceive them? Change is often accompanied by fear, fear of the unknown and fear of the future. What can happen to you that has not already happened? You are most fortunate to be living on the Earth at a time of massive change and growth. But, you also have a great responsibility to make sure that the tools of mass communication are not misused.

Change—for the better or for the worse? You must decide. Many of you are delighted with the toys you have at your disposal. I speak of televisions, video recorders, and computers. A toy for every man, woman, and child on the planet—what a novel concept. Toys can be fun but they can also display images of hatred, bias, and prejudice. Tools of mass communication, people versus people. Will these tools bring an end to the violence that permeates the world? I am not entirely sure that each of you can stand guard against your own needs and desires.

Displays of ego sent across wires, affectionately termed "cyberspace." I must say that many of us who "float" above you are amused. It seems that you need a machine to communicate with one another. Soon, you might think that you can talk to God on the Internet.

So, as you enter the so-called "Third Millennium," ponder this. What changes will the Earth undergo in the next 10 years? The answers to this question and many other intriguing questions can be found in this chapter. Who are you (collectively, as a world) and what have you become?—the age-old questions that many have asked before you. What changes have you undergone in your lifetime? Every person and every thing you encounter and interact with changes your life forever. So, in a changing world, would you expect anything less? (Shamani)

Why have things accelerated so much—technology, information-gathering, the general pace of our lives?

I am sure that to some of you the pace seems unforgiving. Think of what controls the speed and acceleration of technology, information-gathering, and the general pace of your lives. It is the collective consciousness of all souls on the earth plane. As each soul grows, it inherits knowledge and wisdom. One soul communicates a feeling, thought, or idea to another soul. The two souls realize that they share similar feelings, thoughts, and ideas. Their feelings, thoughts, and ideas are communicated to other souls. Soon the collective energy of all these feelings, thoughts, and ideas radiates throughout the universe. The collective energy propels knowledge and wisdom forward at lightning speed.

Think of this, as you learn something, you become more knowledgeable and wise. Then you begin to learn things quicker and tend to focus only on the expected result. I give you the example of your computer technology. Your society has the knowledge and wisdom to create a computer which "thinks" for you. You see that the computer is good but it can be better so you devise ways to make it better. By better, I mean increasing the computer's processing speed. You do not truly understand why it needs to be faster, you only desire it to be faster. So many of you want things to go faster, but what do you really learn? You truly miss the aspect of living.

You can truly have all the technology and information, but unless you recognize and understand what you have and how to use it, it will be of little value to you.

Technology and information-gathering are advanced forms of communication. The knowledge and wisdom you attain through these forms of communication will help you to develop more advanced forms of communication. Simply said, as you increase your knowledge and wisdom collectively, you increase your ability to assimilate more advanced forms of technology and information-gathering into your lives. As you evolve with the technology and information, your ability to utilize it is accelerated.

The general pace of your lives is a function of how you incorporate the advanced forms of technology and information-gathering into your life. The key is to find balance in your life. Do not allow yourself to be taken on a journey to the sun based solely on technology. Think of a scale with two "dishes." In one dish is technology and information-gathering. In the other dish is knowledge and wisdom. If you have too much in one dish, then your life becomes unbalanced. Remember to keep both dishes of your life in balance. You may go as fast or as slow as you want, but always remain balanced. For when you are balanced, you can truly utilize all the technology and information you have. (Asmuth)

How have computers impacted our society?

For better or for worse, let each individual decide. The purple flower appeals to some and not to others. What makes us individual is our ability to see things in our own light. Your truth is not my truth. Your life path is not my life path.

The impact of computers is far-reaching. Many in your society revere them as gods, capable of doing anything.

Computers have allowed you free access to a multitude of images, voices, and sounds. They can never replace the reality of vision, hearing, taste, nor life itself.

Computers are tools which when used for the benefit of all, benefit all.

Computers have been used to build weapons of mass destruction. How many people can you kill—how many lives can you destroy? We all make choices, is this a wise choice? Why do you build such weapons? I say it is out of fear.

Computers have taken people to a new level of awareness. You never realized what was possible, now you only see a glimmer. The mind is much like a computer, but far more complex.

Without the mind, the computer would never exist. Yet your existence depends on it, for better or for worse.

When you "die" (pass over from the earth plane to the next plane), you will not need a computer to do that. Nothing can ever replace the light and your soul's ascension. Never lose sight of your own mind's capacity. You are highly capable of anything you set your mind to.

Computers may make your life easier or more difficult. It depends how you use them. Revere them as gods and they will rule your life.

I see the introduction of computers into your society as a test. It is up to you whether or not you use them, and for what purpose. (Shamani)

What will the Internet give us?

Unlimited access to the greatest thoughts, ideas, and concepts borne in your century. It will open your minds, allowing information to flow freely.

Freedom of expression and ideas carried over a wire. One day you may even converse across the universe.

It cannot replace the need for personal interaction. But I see that it does replace personal interaction. Physical form is of no consequence, there is only a connection of the minds—very interesting since so many in your society place emphasis on the physical (appearance). Now, people must deal with the minds and formulate opinions based on mental interactions. Maybe it is a way for people to get along better. If you can't see a face, you don't know who to be mad at.

The Internet will ultimately teach you how to work together as a collective unit. Communication takes many forms, the Internet is just a stepping stone or an aid to a higher form of communication. Nothing can replace physical interaction. For until people rid themselves of prejudice and bias, words emanating from the mind can be as damaging and destructive as actions of the body. (Shamani)

What do you see as the most important scientific breakthroughs in the near future?

The toys that you play with are often symbols of your true feelings. What can science do that you can not do for yourself? Do you look toward scientific breakthroughs to propel you forward? If you use science in conjunction with proper knowledge and wisdom, you will surely attain the "greatest" scientific breakthroughs of your existence.

The most important scientific breakthroughs will come in the areas of brain and psychic research. Finally, many of you will come to understand the connection between your body, mind, and spirit. Up to now, many of you have viewed those with psychic abilities as being possessed, charlatans, false prophets, and soothsayers. Indeed, there are some who could be labeled in such a way. This is not a time for judgment. Let us focus on those who are purely motivated by love, not by love of fame or fortune. Those of you who have developed the gift of psychic ability shall prosper in the new age. It is important that you share your gift in a loving and positive way for the benefit of all.

Another important scientific breakthrough will be in the area of energy production and transference. The sun is the most powerful energy source that you know of. So why not utilize its true potential? I realize that many of the "persons of power" on the earth plane wish to deter thoughts of such an energy source. But its time has truly come. All can benefit from this source if it is regulated by all for the benefit of all. No one person can own the sun nor its light, so why try?

Within five years, you will find and develop a cure for the so-called "AIDS virus." The cure will be in the form of a combination of a drug and healing affirmations. Medicine and meditation can work hand-in-hand. Look at the ancient cultures who worked with herbs and preparations as well as meditation and prayer to cure ailments and diseases.

The only breakthroughs which should readily concern you are those which you can make in yourself. There are two parts of you, essentially polar opposites. It is important to bring the two parts into balance so that you may become one in body, mind, and spirit. Remember, the tools of science can help or hinder your growth if they are used or not used in conjunction with knowledge and wisdom respectively. (Asmuth)

Are there alternative energy sources and how can we find and develop them?

Yes, oh crystals—beams of light. Pyramids of energy, long ago ancient wisdom, truths untold, secrets revealed.

The great quartz crystal sitting high atop the pyramid. Pyramids of energy—focused on the center. The sun is the eternal giver of life and light. Harness it, use it, develop it.

Each person is a powerhouse of energy, collectively you could light up a city. But in order to do this, you must become pure light, pure energy. Transform your energy into a beam and radiate outward.

Minerals of the earth, givers of light. I hold one up to you—gold in nature, purple when exposed. I speak of copper, a brilliant metal, a great conductor of energy. Mold it into a form—a circle, a square—keep the energy focused. Build with it. The copper pyramid is very powerful. Sit beneath it, focus your energy, become energized with it. A great power source, wireless and without sound. Build them and harness all the power you need. (Asmuth)

Why were we given the tools of film and television?

Film and television, visual aids of communication. A projection of ideas and images to the masses. Mass communication is an art, an art you have learned well.

You have been given these tools for learning. We (on the astral plane) see great benefits through the utilization of these tools. Ideas and thoughts can be conveyed to so many people, people who otherwise could not access the information. These tools allow people to travel around the universe without ever leaving their chair.

The ideas of one can be conveyed to millions. Film and television facilitate the accelerated growth of all things, living and "non-living." Through the positive use of film and television, everyone and everything can benefit. The reality of war and destruction is brought to the forefront of your mind. No longer can people sit in their glass houses and feel protected.

As a person living on the earth at this time, you have an abundance of learning tools. These tools can be used for the benefit or the destruction of all. (Shamani)

How can we use mass communication to benefit society?

Look at the ants, some of the smallest creatures on earth. The ants communicate with each other as they build tunnels beneath the ground. They seem to exemplify the most efficient use of mass communication. Through each individual ant's communication, the entire ant colony benefits.

So I say to you (humans), each of you must communicate with each other for the benefit of everyone. Share your thoughts and ideas. A good idea for social change starts with one person. If that idea is shared with another person and that person shares it with another person, soon everyone will be exposed to that idea. Think—it all started with one person and one idea.

Mass communication is a compilation of many minds, working synchronously. Mass communication, whether it be verbal or telepathic, can effectuate change on a universal level. Thoughts are communicated as energy, the collective energy drives the universe.

Mass communication reaches people in distant places, whether it be geographically or mentally. Without mass communication, we as individuals would have thoughts and ideas lying dormant within ourselves with no outlet.

So I say, today share a thought or an idea and maybe one day it will be communicated back to you. (Shamani)

Why do many of our media representations focus so much on violence and hopelessness?

Destitute souls, souls without purpose. The media representations are a reflection of the violence, despondence, and hopelessness felt by many of you. What you believe in is what you will become.

The media is in the hands of the few. The few make the rules and set guidelines. You will be exposed to their (the few people who control the media) ideas.

The ideas of violence and hopelessness keep many of you focused within. You are seemingly controlled by these ideas. I see that many of you do not even venture out of your homes. You are afraid of that which you see in film and television.

Fear, violence, and hopelessness are all interconnected. So many of you are immobilized by it. You allow something so invisible to control you. When you let it control you, your growth is stunted.

So I say to you, do not allow yourself to be swallowed up by the false power and disguise of violence and hopelessness. Love, peace, and hope wear no disguises. Embrace love, peace, and hope, a reflection for all to see.

When you look at the stars in the nighttime sky, do you not see beauty and hope? Wherever you are, whether it be a high point or a low point in your life, remember the stars are always there. As long as the stars are there, there is hope. (Asmuth)

Why do so many people choose to watch violent television and film?

I ask you, why do so many people pluck feathers from the eagle so that it can not fly? The eagle is a symbol of purity and truth, yet you seek to destroy it. What purpose does it serve?

The path to the truth is very long and arduous if you seek it through violence.

Violence is an affliction of the heart. Do you find self-gratification in hurting yourself or another person? Is your need for violence so prominent that you need to see it over and over again?

You have created outlets for your aggression and violence. Little boxes of terror, televisions and theatres, have been created so that you can act out your violent thoughts and actions.

You feast on the blood and flesh. Your little boxes of terror only serve to remove you from the violence physically. Remember that your thoughts are just as powerful as your actions.

If you truly want peace in the world, lay down your weapons. Cast out violence and replace it with love. Thoughts and acts of love will align you with the truth.

Those who watch violent television and film, you must ask yourself—what if the violence you relish was directed toward someone you love? Would you view it the same? What is the difference?

You may laugh at and mock me for these words. But in these words, there is truth. The question is—are you ready to embrace the truth or will you stand by and watch the violence continue unabated? The choice is yours. (Shamani)

Why has violence become such a part of our lives?

Violence is anger in disguise, and anger is violence in disguise. The disguises you wear—masks of bad intentions. Harm another and you harm yourself. You call it karma.

Your thoughts, the collective energies of a million people trapped in their souls. They are looking for a way out.

Do I feel better seeing another fellow being in pain? What makes me watch the anguish and pain? Celebrate the perpetrators and the perpetration.

Many seek the answers to life's questions through violence. You close your heart so that no one can enter. Are you afraid of what they might see? Keep running from yourself.

Violence like negative emotion can seem as powerful as love and positive emotion. It (violence) wears a unique disguise. You only open yourself to these emotions. We do not dictate your emotions.

There is an absence of love. Love is the answer.

You are what you eat. If you consume violence, you will become it. (Asmuth)

Why is there so much crime?

Crime, victims of rage and anger. Crimes of the heart, how many victims must there be?

Every crime has a story to tell. Most often, it has a tale of destruction. People's lives are forever changed, the last glimmer of hope has faded. Is there hope for peace in the wake of destruction? How many lives must be sacrificed? The sacrificial rites become routine for those who commit the crime and those who are victims.

Crime is a concept used by the powerless to hurt those seemingly in power. Fear is ever present in those who commit the crime, although they profess no fear. Fear runs rampant among many of you. There seems to be no end in sight. People run helplessly along the streets. "Will I be next?" are the words I often hear.

Crime is fueled by the thoughts and energies of many people. Many of these people are unhappy with their lives. If people were happy, and respected and loved themselves and other people, there would be no crime. Until then, you must not be controlled by the thoughts and energies of the few (those who commit the crimes). You must put your strength in supporting loving and positive actions. If you focus on glorifying crime, then you only have yourself to ask, "Why is there so much crime?" (Shamani)

What should we tell our children about crime and violence?

Blades and fire consume many souls. There are many who wield the sword of death with great intent and purpose. They hide behind a shield of insecurity. How long can they hide—the truth must be known. I say to those people, cast your swords aside and lay down your shields. How many people do you have to hurt before you see that the hate you feel lies within you?

You can not blame others for your feelings of rage and anger. The more you hide behind your shield or run away, the more enraged you become. Do you doubt your ability to love and do good things? Why don't you reach out to another human being for assistance, but do it out of love for that person and most importantly, yourself. You are the keeper of your soul. The body you have chosen to carry your soul must be kept whole.

I say to the children, remember love is the answer to all that plagues the world. There are some people who wear shields or protective armor to mask their true emotions and insecurity. Do not be drawn into the energy of crime and violence, it has false power. Crime and violence do not stand true in the light.

I say to the parents of the children, be an example to your children. Show them how to love and respect all life. Teach them to positively express themselves. Feelings must be expressed, give them an outlet. You are responsible in part for their soul's development. I see many children focused on a screen (television and video games). I ask you, why do they sit here, unmonitored? The images they see are filled with crime and violence. But you say your society is filled with crime and violence. It is not only the food you feed your children that helps them grow. By allowing your children to watch crime and violence on the screen, you are creating a future based on that which you detest.

Teach the children the value of life, for your future depends on it. (Asmuth)

Why do we often feel like victims?

Pyramids stand high, a purpose higher than ourselves. Riddles to the few, questions unanswered, sights unseen.

Crimes of passion. Victims stand alone, stiff in the wind, unbeknownst to many. Visibly cursed, life without purpose. Retrieve thy self, the eagle speaks in soft tones. Listen and understand. Come seek the answers—a thousand questions, a thousand answers. (Shamani)

How do we release our "victim" self-image?

Release through expression. Self-expression yearns for guidance. Guided by the light down a long dark road. Who knows what lies ahead. Dormant ideas, expressions unnoticed, paths not yet taken.

Examine the self, what is your purpose? Life seems dismal, you are carried along. Do not come looking for answers, the answers are locked within. Go within and seek that which makes you prominent within yourself. Self-preservation is the key, unlock the doors to your soul. Proclaim your innocence, your self-indulgence, your dignity.

Express yourself and be one with it. It can only be what you make of it. The desires are strong, we find one to blame but find a blameless heart. The key is to love oneself beyond imagine. Imagine all that is good, all that can be. Embrace and embody the goodness. Goodness reigns within each of us.

Feathers of white, oh pearly white, plucked one by one, reveal your true self. Rise up and celebrate who you are. See the purpose of your life, one who holds the key to eternity.

Life without victims, life without proverb. Proverbs bring us to the crystalline mountaintop, the mountaintop of life. The spirit fully expressed through nature and form. Reach the epitome of life, the purpose is clear but sometimes lacks direction. It is for you I wish this. For this is true expression of the self. You deserve it, let no one tell you otherwise. You are the director of your life. Life without purpose is life without form. The eagle focuses intently on the purpose at hand, devoid of . . . (Shamani)

What would you say to those doing criminal acts?

To you I say, lay down your weapons. Not only your guns and knives but your hands. Who is it that you wish to hurt, yourself or someone else?

Take off the mask you wear, let me see your face. I see the life you have been given. I see the scars you have. I feel the pain in your mind. But I ask you, for what purpose have you inflicted pain on another soul?

When you look in the mirror, what do you see? Are you afraid of what you might see?

You have a choice. You can choose a cycle of crime which takes you nowhere, you always come back to the same point. Or you can choose to confront the issues of change. Do you want to change? The choice is yours. (Shamani)

Why was the gun invented?

Objects of fantasy or objects of reality? What is a gun but a weapon of control and destruction? Are those who use guns emotionally secure? Can inner security be replaced by a symbol of superficial security? It seems those who invented the gun thought so.

"Why was the gun invented?" you ask. It was initially invented under the disguise of protecting people from animals. But as you now see, guns are generally used to protect people from people. The problem is guns are in the hands of many. When guns are in the hands of many, there are many people walking around in fear. Guns were invented to squelch that fear. As you can see, what you fear is what you become.

Guns create a false sense of security. The bigger the gun, the more secure you feel. Who has the biggest gun?—two opposing sides have argued this for years. Which side will admit they have the biggest gun? If one side admitted this, then the other side would attempt to make a bigger gun. Would this side feel more or less secure with a bigger gun? The bigger the gun, the greater the fear. And so the argument continues—who has the biggest gun?

Can I ask you one question, does it really matter? Guns are tools which can be used to maim or destroy one or many lives. How can guns promote peace when you let guns do the talking? Does a gun conjure up images of love and peace? Guns only protect you from your own fears and insecurities. The bullets that are ejected from your guns are filled with these fears and insecurities.

Remember, one person invented the gun. Now look at the global implications of one person's fears and insecurities. See how one life choice can impact the lives of many. Make your choices wisely, for the consequences of those choices may reach far beyond your life. (Asmuth)

Why do we have war?

War of the minds, war of the souls—where does it stop? "Stop the war" is a familiar cry I hear. Cries for help, destitute minds, skin peeled off, blood shed all over. Cries of the innocent—when will it ever end? Do you learn from war? Yes, but the lessons need not be so difficult.

Egos, yours and mine—how do we resolve the conflict? Pick up a gun and blow each other away. Where is the sense in this? What did it solve? Did your souls communicate? If they did, fear would be most prominent next to anger. Why must anger move to the forefront? How self-destructive. Destruction at the hands of a few, darkness chosen over light.

When will the day come when you have no need for these trials by fire? Fire consumes everything, it leaves no prisoners. Those left behind to view the destruction are devastated. Think of the children, they are your hope and promise for the future. A future without guns and missiles is what we ask of you. Can you survive without them? (Asmuth)

What is the meaning of the war in Bosnia?

Guns, fretfulness, fulfilling to some. See the poverty, the oppression, would you not fight for what you believe is right? (Asmuth)

How can we end war altogether?

You can end war altogether by acknowledging and understanding that there is no need for war. If you say that war is necessary to maintain security and stability, then I say that you dwell in the depths of insecurity. What is a war but a battle of egos?

If you are secure with your own identity and position in life, then you will see no need to challenge others to do battle. It is imperative that each and every citizen of the world realizes and understands this simple answer. I challenge every one of you to become secure with yourself.

The battles you wage have no winners or losers, but many casualties. Wars have been waged on earth since the time humans inhabited the earth. Don't you think that after thousands of years, peace would inevitably evolve out of war? Indeed, peace has been rendered across the earth, time and time again. But alas, new battles and new wars are waged. If they handed out medals for insecurity, there would be no one left to fight the wars. Do you understand what I am saying?

Many of you think of the collective wars your nations wage against others. But I ask you to think of the individual battles and wars you wage with yourself, your family, your coworkers, and nature. All of these individual battles and wars contribute to the collective consciousness of war. If you say there are no world wars at present, then why are the world's inhabitants (you) at war against each other?

Once you understand what the root cause of war is, then you must focus on a positive solution. Peace starts with you—one voice, one body, one mind, and one spirit. Start by trying to accept and love yourself. It does not matter what others might think of you. I will tell you that you are the most beautiful person in the world and so is everyone else. Remember, from "one" you were conceived and to "one" you shall return. Simply said, we are all one. We are all segments of "one," try to respect each other's diversity.

Learn to accept yourself as a single entity with a single purpose, and recognize and accept others' rights to the same. For the peace that you seek in yourself is no different than the peace others seek in themselves. You can end war altogether by choosing peace. So I ask you, are you first willing to make peace with yourself? Peace will bring security and stability, and security and stability will bring peace. Are you ready to accept it? (Shamani)

Why do accidents and disasters happen?

Those things that do not stand true in the light are subject to these events. When we do not follow our true purpose or stray from our life path, we open ourselves. Our course is changed forever.

Accidents and disasters are lessons in disguise. How you recover from these is the true test. Obstacles and challenges help us to grow. Growth is a learning process. We all have lessons, some we may grow tired of. When we resist the flow, we are subject to these accidents and disasters. There are no coincidences.

Wisdom comes through learning and following your life path. Stray from the path and you will be led back to it.

For some, this may sound cold and callous. If you find yourself affected by an accident or a disaster, think of what you can learn. Is this the way to higher truth?

All questions need answers. All questions have answers but sometimes the answers are not simple. The answers are often disguised in ordinary things. (Asmuth)

What would you say to those who lost their homes in the hurricanes?

Skies of terror opened unleashing rain and wind. The oceans rose to meet the land. Nature does not discriminate, nature is everywhere. It knows no boundaries. The earth is a very complex system. You have not even begun to understand the complexity. The earth is not something you can rule. You can not control it.

The houses you build are boxes which you place yourself in. You seek protection from the elements (wind, rain, and snow) and other people. You have lost the sense of community and of working together. You stay in your little boxes, watching the world revolve around you. You are safe in this notion until disaster strikes. Then you see the truth. You see strangers helping strangers, neighborhoods working together for a common cause. But where is this attitude the rest of the time? Why does it often take a disaster to bring people together?

You must feel humble now. When you are stripped of everything you own, even your clothes, you stand alone and naked. At this point, you are forced to look at yourself and within yourself. What do you see?

Rebuild you will, it may take a long time. You will survive, you always have, you always will. But I ask you to think about what you are rebuilding. Are you just rebuilding your house or will you rebuild yourself also?

Opportunities for growth are often disguised. What will you learn from this experience?

Things can be replaced—we can do without a lot of things. But life is more precious and sacred—can it be readily replaced? No!

So, I ask you to ponder the life you have been given. Live the way of the truth, and the truth shall come to thee. (Asmuth)

Why do so many people crave drama in their lives?

Drama is creative expression of the human spirit.

The road to knowledge and wisdom is fairly straight and smooth. Although there are minor bumps and holes, the road is not impassable. Many of you who crave drama in your lives wish to make the journey more difficult than it is. Instead of keeping a clear vision of what lies ahead, you become distracted and fall over the bumps and into the holes. Feeling insecure and embarrassed, you tell tales of deep crevasses and tall mountains that you have traversed. You become impassioned and tell the tale to anyone who will listen. Soon, you draw a crowd, your ego grows as big as the tale you tell. Every word from your mouth hinges on the last. You say, let the drama unfold. Now, you are so caught up in the drama that you can't escape.

The deep crevasses and tall mountains that you have created now stand in the way. You have trapped yourself in your own creation. Your life is an inescapable drama. Drama is only an escape from what is real, the truth. Those who crave drama in their lives are not honest with themselves. You know who you are. Your life can be as dramatic or melodramatic as you desire. Remember that your desires create drama in your life.

I ask you to maintain a vision of who you truly are. Align yourself with the road that leads to knowledge and wisdom. All the drama you need awaits those who are willing to discover their inner selves. (Asmuth)

What will we learn in the next twenty years?

You will learn how to derive simplicity from complexity. Living a simpler existence is necessary for your survival. Those of you who can learn this simple lesson will fully prosper in the coming years.

You will also learn how to heal yourself of many ailments and diseases. Affirmations and meditation are the keys which will help you. So many of you do not see the gift of healing that you have. I invite each of you to be responsive to your own healing ability. Remember the road to wellness starts with you.

You will learn the true meaning of living in peace. Discourses on war will be prevalent in history classes. The children who are born twenty years from now will only be able to read about war as if it never existed. Many of you fear the future, for you feel war is certain. I ask you to lay down your "arms" (your guns, missiles, and bombs). What purpose do they have but to separate each of you? Peace is a reality for most of the world (earth plane). Are you ready to declare peace in your world?

The next twenty years will surely be filled with challenges. You may choose a path that no others have chosen. There are always leaders and followers. If you choose the path to the light and truth, others will follow you. There will be those who deny the truth. For them the path will be very difficult, unless they accept what has been written.

I challenge each of you to align yourself with your higher purpose. If you are not sure what your higher purpose is, let your past be your guide. What difficult lessons have you had to learn in the past? Are you repeating the same lessons over and over in terms of your career, life, and relationships? Take time to ask yourself, who am I? Am I happy with who I am? Do I love myself? You may see that you are forcing life upon yourself. You are the key to your higher purpose.

Twenty years from now, you will look back in pure amazement. You will see that the answers to life's most important questions were right in front of you. Now, you have the knowledge and wisdom of this book to assist you in your journey. The rest is up to you. I wish you good fortune today and always. Let the magic in your soul illuminate your life path. (Asmuth)

What will happen to the earth plane as we approach the year 2000?

A new millennium awaits your discovery. A countenance of options lie before you. There are many prophets among you who speak of death and destruction. Many a false prophet rule the world (the earth plane). Those who listen to these false prophets surely are confused and wallow in their own pity. Surely it is a pity that you must ask this question. Many civilizations before you led themselves down similar paths. They too pondered their fate, the fate of a thousand years.

So many of you see time as the ruler of your fate. The thoughts and energy you give time may well determine your fate. Is time of the essence, or is the essence in time? Ponder this question, the answers you seek concerning your fate can be found in this question.

Look to no others to save you from yourself. The angels of mercy watch over and guide you, but you (collectively as humans) ultimately must decide your own fate. Will it be worldwide pestilence, fear, famine, catastrophes, and abominations or worldwide love, beauty, honesty, respect, care, and unity? The choice seems easy, doesn't it? Then I ask, why do so many of you refuse to embrace the latter? What are you afraid of?

The earth has many scars from your civilizations as well as past civilizations. If you choose to abandon the earth plane, what legacy are you leaving? And who will be around to hear it? All of you have been given the gift of eternal life, so why not preserve it? Be a symbol of hope and love for others to see.

The earth plane can be saved from the words of the soothsayers and false prophets. However, the thoughts and words of love must come from each of you. The foundation of love has been laid, and each of you symbolize bricks of love. The building cannot stand tall and true if one brick is missing. Each of you is responsible for the fate of the earth plane.

Mine are words of truth, not words of a prophet. I ask you not to look at the year 2000 as an end but as a new beginning. This I will say, the year 2000 will be a "time" of people helping people. The year 2000 will be the start of a new millennium and the manifestation of the collective human spirit. Will the collective human spirit embrace "life" or "death"? Each of you must decide! (Asmuth)

Chapter 11:

Answers To Questions You Might Not Ask

Difficult answers to difficult questions, where do the answers come from? Questions you might not ask are surely questions that need to be asked. The questions are as important as the answers. But I ask you, why do these questions need to be asked? Do you resist the temptations of the world? Do you look for perfection in everything on Earth? Judge the sick, the impaired, the dying, the living, the adventurers, the poor, the rich, the richest of the poor, the poorest of the rich, and all people and things in between.

People and things, what's the difference? It's only your perception of your own weakness of spirit. Take a long ride down a short road, where does it get you? You end up where you started from, asking difficult questions which have simple answers. The simple answer is love, that which reigns supreme over all things. But, love is not superior, it is only a manifestation of the spirit of each and every thing in the universe. Remember, we are all one, distinctions and differences are the product of your own insecurity with your own life.

If you truly love yourself, look at yourself in the mirror and ask yourself, why do I find fault with others and myself? This is a difficult question to answer, I'm sure!

So I invite you to read on into this chapter and discover what it is in you that makes you ask these difficult questions. The answers may surprise you, but the truth often wears many disguises. Read between the lines of truth and discover the truth about who you are. Open your mind and soul to receive the gift of life. Once you have received it, open yourself and share the gift with others.

Believe in yourself, you are truly blessed with the light and truth. May you find oneness in yourself, separate from yourself no longer. For once you have become aware, you can never turn back. Remember, six months from now, one year from now, you will look back and say: I know that love has touched my life and I am forever changed by the questions I might have never asked. (Asmuth)

Why do we have so many addicted people at this time?

Surely you realize that addiction is a sign of a weakness in spirit. Those of you who do not embrace the spirit of yourself do a disservice to the spirit of your ancestors. Your ancestors have paved the way for you to learn. They endured many hardships and sacrificed their lives so that you could have a better life.

And so, many of you have determined that you want to capture life and live in a world of addiction. But I ask you, has not life captured you? Where did the addiction begin? Can you blame your addictions on your ancestors through genetic implications, or can you blame your addictions on societal decay? For once, you might entertain the thought that you are the source of your addiction. No one can force dependent behavior on an independent person. Are you a dependent or independent person—what role do you play? Do you play your role out of convenience or dependence?

When did your addiction begin—as a child or as an adult? When will it end? The answer is when you choose to face your addiction. Each of you is addicted to something—you can not deny this. I speak not of just alcohol or drugs, but also of work, sports, recreation, television, video games, support groups, unhealthy behavior patterns, and the list goes on and on.

You have chosen the addictions and the consequences of those addictions. But you can also choose to become aware of your addictions, surround them with love, and release them. Seek to embrace the spirit of yourself through a love for yourself. You are a beautiful person and can set yourself free from that which holds you a prisoner to yourself—your addictions. You have the strength in body, mind, and spirit—are you willing to use it? (Shamani)

What would you say to people using drugs?

Drugs, whether labeled illegal or legal, are still body- and mind-altering substances. The way you choose to use drugs determines whether there will be adverse effects or not. You can choose to let a drug control you and your life. It is not the drug that makes you perform better or worse, it is the power you give to that drug. If you pledge allegiance to the country and the drugs it produces, you are just as responsible as the so-called drug peddler or user.

Do not disillusion yourself about the drugs you use. You may think that you are helpless without the drugs. In some cases of terminally-ill people, I might agree. But for most of you, drugs are treated as a source of escape from the perceived misery and pain of your life. Too often, I hear the phrase, "life sucks and then you die." Well I say, you have chosen to live your life according to this phrase.

Are drugs creators of fact or fantasy? You decide. There is a place for drugs in your society, but only if those who use them are educated properly. Herbal medicines and remedies may be considered less intrusive on the body and mind. They may not produce the elevated state of body or mind that you desire, but then does the drug produce it?

I ask those of you who use drugs, whether labeled illegal or legal, to ask yourself, what does the drug give me that I am not capable of giving myself? You will find that you are not capable of loving yourself. The disease and sickness does not make you ill, it is your denial of love for yourself. Indeed many of you may choose to continue using drugs even after you read this. That is your choice, but remember, sooner or later you will have to face yourself because the road to escape always leads to a dead end. (Shamani)

Where did "crack cocaine" come from?

Look in the olive garden. See the green olives, where did they come from? The "greenbacks" haunt many of you. You are bound by the laws of money. There is a huge division between those of you who have money and those who do not. Those who do not have money sought to "even" the score, so to speak. I speak of illustrious mansions, waterfront homes, exotic cars, things of fantasy to be purchased so as to enter the higher echelons of greed. For do not many of you equate money with power? But I say to you, are you more powerful or powerless? Does money guide you along the path to the truth and light? Or are you just a time traveler taking a non-stop, one-way trip to death and destruction?

Look at what you as an individual have. What are you contributing to the universe, is it for your higher good or your higher "gold"? Gold pieces can buy many objects of fancy and fantasy, but what do they buy you? Can you buy more time on the earth plane? When you think you can, think again!

Deserters of faith are often looked upon as failures. Where does the failure lie, within you or someone else? Is this a question or an answer? Is it fact or fiction? I let you decide. Each of you holds your personal fate in your hands. But, which hand is it? I ask you to join both hands, see what two can do! When you see what two can do, open your hands to help others. Do not look to be compensated for what you do not have, rejoice in what you have.

So I say to each of you, "crack cocaine" originated with greed. Now, it is up to each of you to discover where greed fits into your individual life. Greed is not only monetary but social. Deviant behavior does not start in the home, it starts with the individual.

You can say that "crack cocaine" is a curse but then each of you is admonished of guilt. It is a product of your culture, it has a beginning and an end. May you discover its end by recognizing and understanding its beginning. (Asmuth)

What would you say to someone using "crack"?

Beguiled by the terror, you wish to stray from the path of higher learning. You can do no greater disservice to yourself than ingesting "drugs of fantasy." What is it that you seek to escape from? Is it yourself—is your life that pitiful and devoid of love? Where is it that you seek to be, is it demons you seek? If so, you will only find them in yourself.

It is you who make and break the rules, it is your life, your choices. Make no one else responsible for your choices. You can choose death or life, I can only watch. I can feel no pain for you because you feel no pain yourself. It is you and only you who can say yes or no. I can only advise you, you must determine what is right for you.

Abuse the body, abuse the mind, abuse the spirit. All of you is affected.

There is HOPE, but it can only start with you. I dare say that the birds in the trees may soon sing sweet lullabies to you. You will hear them but you will not be awake. When can you remember the last time you awakened from a good night's sleep? Sleep is not what you seek but it may find you. Will you be ready?

Are you ready to accept your life? There is so much you have to give, but you do not recognize it. Take off your sunglasses and the blindfold beneath them. You can no longer hide from the truth, for you are an embodiment of the truth.

The stars you see in your eyes represent your destiny. What is your destiny—do you know? Open your eyes, the world has changed so much. Are you willing to be a part of it? The illusions you have are real in your state of mind. I do not deny what you see. But I ask you, do you want to remain in a drug-induced illusion? Are you ready to acknowledge that you have power over a chemical produced by "man" to destroy "man"?

There is a life beyond the cookie- and candy-coated substance you call "crack." Do not let your desires make you weak, find the strength within yourself to say "No!" You have the strength and power to rise above that which you give your life to. Give life to yourself, you will soon see that the greatest gift of all is the renewed life you have given yourself.

Remember that you are not alone, there are those on earth and those who watch over you. We all love you and are always with you. Open your heart and let the love flow in. Fill yourself and help others to find the way to love and truth. We wish you the best in your journey to wellness. Remember, you are not alone. (Asmuth)

Why do so many children have life-threatening illnesses?

Sunlight always shines through the darkest clouds. I ask you to remember that all children are special. I realize that you have difficulty understanding why some children have life-threatening illnesses. You ask, why are some children touched with illness while others are seemingly untouched? Karmic lessons are often at the root of life-threatening illnesses. The karmic lessons may involve the child alone, the parents, a caretaker, or any others who are connected with the child. I caution you not to blame the child, yourself, nor anyone else.

There are many sacrifices each soul must make in order to elevate oneself to higher levels of consciousness. A life-threatening illness often enables a soul to deal with its karmic lessons at an accelerated rate. An illness which threatens a life also humbles the person. A child or adult is taken to the inner core of who they are.

I ask you to remember that all of you have eternal life. Your life on the earth plane may seem limited but you may return in another form (another body or being). There are many of you who have been on the earth plane before. You know of the words "deja vu." You have memories of past lives. Remember why you are here—to deal with the "past."

I ask you to see illness not as life-threatening but life-enriching. Enrich your life with love and share it with all the children, young and old, in the universe. The beauty of love always shines upon you. Accept your soul's lessons and you shall forever be enriched with love and life. (Shamani)

What would you say to someone who has lost a child?

The loss you feel now bears no comparison. You may feel anger and pain now, you have a right to express these feelings. No one can begin to understand your personal grief, though those who love you may try. I say it is important to communicate your feelings to a friend or lover, someone you love and trust. This may help to ease some of the pain and anguish. But, if you are not ready to do this, do not force yourself. For in time, you shall come to this point again.

Can I ask you not to blame yourself or the child? Although you may not realize it now, there is a higher purpose in all things. There are few random events on the earth plane. There is structure in a seemingly confused and disoriented universe. I ask you to trust the universe, for it will provide all of what you need. You must only ask and believe.

The loss of your child may be one of the lowest points of your life. The loss of anyone you love can be devastating emotionally, mentally, physically, and spiritually. Who can predict an untimely death or separation?

You may feel that all the pieces of your life are scattered around now. But, remember there is always hope for an emotional, mental, physical, and spiritual recovery. Love will help to guide you through the maze of feelings. The intensity of the pain will not last forever, this I can assure you.

If your child has "passed over to the other side," be assured that he or she is "alive" and well. The same angels that watch over you also watch over your child. Your child is forever protected in the light. One day, you will join him or her in the garden of paradise. Until that time, please find comfort in my words. The words I speak are for you alone to hear.

For those of you who have lost a child through a separation or divorce, or simply alcohol or drugs, I speak to you also. I ask, who has lost touch with whom? Is it you—the parent or the child? Love and respect are partners in communication. If you communicate both of these, there can be no separation. Though you might be physically separated from each other, no one can deny your mental and spiritual connection. Relationships are based on trust—where there is trust, there is love!

As difficult as it is for you to accept that you have "lost" your child, it is even more difficult for your child to accept that he or she has lost you. In most cases, you who are older are much more knowledgeable and wiser. And so it is your responsibility to impart some of that knowledge and wisdom upon your child.

When someone feels emotional pain, their first instinct is to run from it. If you run too fast, you may stumble and hurt yourself further. Then you must recount your steps and confront your emotions once again. Wouldn't it be better to face your emotions head on? I realize this may be beyond your ability but I only ask you to think about it.

Preserve your self-identity, for this is what you can lean on in your time of loss. Please remember that love has no boundaries. The spirit of your child and you are forever connected in love. (Asmuth)

Why do we have child abuse?

The children so indiscriminately cast aside. All the hopes and dreams shattered. The crystal ball of terror, a future filled with gloom and doom. The faces of children etched in memories. The memories could have been brighter, had the light been allowed to shine in.

Jealousy and outrage directed toward an innocent life. Is it superiority that the abuser feels? Is it a lack of self-control? Has the anger and blame of oneself been unjustly directed onto the face or body of a child?

Whether verbal or physical abuse, there is no difference. Both leave scars of pain and indifference. Sometimes, the wounds run so deep that the pain and grief never subside.

You ask—can there be justice in a world of injustice?

Until people learn to cast out the self-proclaimed demons of hate, jealousy, greed, selfishness, and blame, child abuse will continue. The abused will become the abusers and the abusers will become the abused. The cycle continues as sad as it is.

Remember that the cycle doesn't have to continue, you can make the choice. Do not cast yourself in the role of the abused or the abuser. Take a stand and stand by yourself. Be a symbol of love and allow yourself to be loved. (Asmuth)

How can we stop the abuse of children—individually and collectively?

Take off the mask of insecurity and inadequacy—stop projecting blame onto the child for your own feelings of inadequacy and insecurity. Project a more positive role as a parent or a teacher. If you allow the abuse to continue, then you accept responsibility for the consequences. As I said before, do not cast yourself in a script as the abused or the abuser.

The pain is immeasurable. How long must the children cry before someone listens? There are too many deaf ears and deaf hearts.

The abused individual must stand firm. Do not let your spirit be weakened or broken. The hands or voices of cruelty may cast a spell over you. But believe that the spell can be broken. The magic of love still shines within you, open yourself to it, you so richly deserve it.

The individual who abuses another should not be cast out in shame. Shame is for those who cannot stand on their own. You must ask yourself—why do you abuse the child? Were you abused as a child? You must read and internalize the words of the preceding paragraph. Until you break the cycle, you not only hurt the child but you hurt yourself. Learn to balance your anger and jealousy—there is no need to blame. Reach out for help—you do not have to make the journey alone. Once you face yourself, then the healing can begin. A new beginning, devoid of abuse for yourself or another.

Collectively, you must show support for each other. I ask you to forgive each other, do not draw lines in the sand. If you try to ignore what is going on, you are only running from the truth. I assure you the truth waits for you around the corner. Education and understanding will help prevent child abuse. Educate your children and the adults. (Asmuth)

Why are so many children being abducted?

The owl speaks to you in words you can understand. In order to understand why children are being abducted, you must first look into the eyes of a child. What do you see but innocence and purity? There are those that wish to regain the feelings of innocence and purity. They have not matured beyond the childhood stage, it seems as if they are being held prisoner by their own childhood.

Abduction of a child by a parent is generally based on envy. In a child-custody battle, one parent seemingly "wins" the love of the child while the other parent "loses." So if a parent can not find justice in the justice system, then individual justice is rendered. Who loses but the child? The seeds of love and trust are planted in the mind of the child but are slow to grow or never grow.

In the case of a "stranger" abducting a child, you must first understand that the abductor only has his or her self-interests in mind. Illusion and trickery are often used to lure unsuspecting children. These people often know the language of the children and are essentially adults trapped in a child's mind.

The number one reason why children are being abducted is for money. Those who abduct children are motivated by the color green and all it can buy. Children are often bought and sold like commodities. Those who commit these offenses against children are indeed weak in spirit. They seek the children to renew themselves with strength. Control is the only tool they have and if they lose control, they have no power so to speak.

I do not wish to focus any more energy in this direction. I see a lot of pain surrounding the children and their families.

Let it suffice to say that you should tell your children how to protect themselves. Do not hide the truth about abduction from them. Let your children know that you love them dearly. Spend time with your children. Violence is seemingly a large part of your society. If you let your children interact with violence on a daily basis through television and video games, you are only supporting the violence you condone.

Speak to your children in words that they can understand. Remember what it was like to be a child, many moons have risen and set since then. But the ideas of love and respect are still the same. Find a way to treat the ills of society. Start by teaching your children the power of positive thinking. Positive change can only occur when several minds envision positive actions and results. Abduction and violence should never be viewed as the norm. The cycle of violence can be broken, it starts with you. (Shamani)

What would you say to someone who abducts a child?

Mountains of misery should not be projected onto a child. Indeed, your childhood was filled with pain and misery. Now, why do you wish to inflict the same upon an innocent child? Child abduction is a most serious offense to the child's soul and your soul. You seemingly prey on the weak to strengthen yourself. But I say to you, you are truly weak in all aspects of your being. You may call me to judgment, but what I voice is the truth.

Who do you love in the world? Do you love your mother, father, sisters, brothers, and/or friends? Were they not children at one time? How would you have felt if you or one of them were abducted? So how can you deny the hurt and pain you inflict on the child and those who love the child?

You can not hold others responsible for your failures in life. I don't acknowledge that you are a failure, you have made certain choices and learned by them. I ask you to release the child in yourself and the child you have abducted. Who are you that can give and take life? Do you wish to play the role of "God" or another "supreme entity"?

Find a way to forgive yourself for who you are and what you have become. Release the child unharmed and give the child what you do not respect—life! I ask you to either remove yourself far away from children, as in a desolate and remote location, or seek help from a professional trained in psychology. In either case, you must seek to help yourself. The child in you is alive and well, do not seek to destroy it or the life of another.

Love is not absent from your life, only your perception of it. If you hate yourself, do not project your hatred onto others. You are responsible for your life on the earth plane, I ask you to love and respect all things, living and non-living. Above all, love and respect yourself. For if you do, you will forever release yourself from the pain and misery that you are feeling now. The healing must begin with the child and adult within you. (Asmuth)

Why is there pornography?

Pornography exists in the minds of those who wish to devalue their own spirit. Each of you has lusted or desired something in your life. Look upon those who practice pornography in the same light. Theirs is a desire for self-gratification through sexual means. You may label this deviant behavior—you are well within your rights. But remember that you are one who desires and lusts for other things.

Pornography is viewed as an art form. The human body is objectified so that you may attain sexual gratification. Pornography is an unpure form of love. Those who view pornography do not see the magic of love. It is simply a deviation from the essence of love.

Those who read or view pornography feel a sense of control. But does not the book or film provoke that person to a controlled act? There is no need to control others through sexual acts. Sex should not be viewed as a game of control. Those who seek control over others have no control at all. The weak in spirit prey on the strong, and the strong become the subjects and objects of the weak.

Subjectify and objectify, these are disguises of pornography. Learn to recognize them in yourself and others. Once you recognize them, then ask yourself—why is there pornography? (Asmuth)

Why do men rape? What would you say to someone who has been raped?

When you rape the mind, you rape the body! Men feel the need to maintain superiority over their environment. Out of this is born feelings of inadequacy and insecurity. Their maleness is threatened to the point where some men seek a way to vent their frustrations. Most often their frustrations find an outlet which is directed at women. It is easy for them to blame another person for their own feelings of inadequacy and insecurity.

For those women and children who have been raped, I give you each a purple robe to wear. May the healing process begin. Do not blame yourself for what happened. You are not to blame. It is important that you open yourself up and communicate your feelings of hate, anger, and mistrust. The healing can only begin when you are ready.

Remember, men who rape are weak in spirit. They prey on those who are strong. In their minds, they are strong, preying on the weak. I realize these words may not comfort you. I say again, the healing must begin with you. Love shared between two consenting souls can be the most beautiful, spiritually uplifting experience. Open yourself to heal and to the love you so richly deserve. (Asmuth)

Has there always been violence?

The idea of violence started with the thought of one being. There is love in violence but the idea of love is expressed in a lackluster way. Remember that everything is one. Violence is an offshoot of love, it is only expressed in a manner that is not conducive to true growth.

Violence is a choice, just like love. Those who use violence as a means of hurting others only hurt themselves. Those who use violence to induce death are far removed from their souls. Violence is perpetuated by the thoughts of many. Violence is a form of energy. Remember that energy can be very powerful, it only has the power you give it.

Violence is a control mechanism. When you inflict verbal or physical violent energy on another person or thing, you feel control but you are out of control. So where is the balance?

Remember that from one thought, violence was born. To this I say, you can choose to perpetuate the violence or diffuse the thoughts of violence. There is only false power and false love in violence. Replace your thoughts of violence with thoughts of love and understanding. (Asmuth)

Why was Martin Luther King, Jr., killed?

To support the weapons of mass destruction. A man who so believed in himself, a symbol of honesty and truth. A trusting soul, he paved the way for success. To strip the defiance from its statue, which stood so long. However, defiled, disgraced, beleaguered, left to die in a reign of terror. A sacrifice to all who knew him. Honesty, integrity—can sadness be replaced with happiness? The pain lashes out against the terror. Terror of a few who saw defiance reigning.

Cause without purpose. Death without reason. All must come to an end whereby a new beginning is born. Cast out self-doubt, sometimes truth reigns in terror. Seek to strip away the disguise, the hatred. Equality and life for all. Let no man or woman take another's life. (Asmuth)

What would you say to the relatives of a murder victim?

The white and gold robes I wear are symbolic of my love for you. I realize at this moment in time you seek many answers to many questions. Your faith in God may be called into question. The answers you seek can be found in reading this book, focus on the chapters of love and family. You will surely find many words of inspiration and love in the questions as well as the answers.

No one can bring back the physical body of your loved one. However, the love you have for the one you have lost transcends the boundaries between "life" and "death." Please know that the love you still feel reaches beyond the earth plane and touches the one you are seemingly separated from. They feel the love which you so graciously share with them. They want you to know that they return the same amount of love. The separation has caused them some anxiety and pain. But where they are is a place filled with love and peace. They ask that you find the same on Earth.

Murderers and victims, we are one in the same, and we are both seeking to find the love we have been separated from. Can we forgive each other and renew ourselves in love and peace? The universal essence of love and peace shines upon all of us. I hope that you can find the path to love and peace so that we will no longer separate ourselves into murderers and victims. If not for yourself, do it for your children! (Asmuth)

What do we do, collectively, with people who murder?

Send them to the light, the purple robes of passion shall be restitution. They have to answer for their misguidance. You cannot be responsible for diluting their minds. Justice is in the eye of the beholder. Vigor and might will not teach them. They must find the way to eternal life. Although many lives they have taken, bless them and send them on their way. All who seek forgiveness are healed in the light. (Asmuth)

What do we do—individually and collectively—to help these souls?

Individually, seek forgiveness for your own misgivings. Again, you are not responsible for their trials and tribulations. Seek out the truth for yourself. Once you find it, share it with others. Through living, you become an example for all to see.

Collectively, envision a better world. World problems are full of misguided souls. The Hitlers who once ruled the world (Earth) are no longer here but remain in our minds as a tribute. I can not admonish these actions.

I know many are saddened and angry. Honesty, a travesty to sin, no one can bring back the horror that you (these segments of society) feel—it is locked in a cavern. Let these people be a symbol of the collective consciousness. Collectively, we are all one. Scorn one and you scorn yourself. To this end, this is true.

Forgive yourself for this travesty against humanity. Forgiveness comes from within. To thine own self be true. Truth is what you make of it. It is not holy or destitute—sort of a riddle and until you solve the riddle, all of life seems peculiar.

The violets are red, chrysanthemums blue. But out (absent) of the light, all appears the same. I am philosophical by nature but that is what I am—true to myself.

Clavis per unum. The truth lies within—go seek it, then return to me. (Asmuth)

In what ways do these people help or benefit us?

You are healed by their actions. Without rhyme or reason, a means to an end. The collective consciousness centers on each and every action of each and every soul in the universe. Judge not yet ye be judged is a familiar phrase passed down and commonly used.

Serenity in a pool exists even when a rock is thrown into the pool. The ripple effect is synchronous. To this end, even though a soul thrashes about, the pool still stands still. Gorillas in the wild seem to disturb the other animals, until nighttime falls and all is quiet.

Peace in the wilderness, the forest is green, abundant growth. Only a pebble thrown in the vastness can thirst. See the vastness and realize, truth in learning lies within the vastness. (Asmuth)

What happens to the souls of criminals and murderers after they leave the earth plane?

They join the collective consciousness. There is no distinction. Earth is to sky as sky is to earth. It is all one. Soul is to the body as the body is to the soul.

Lessons to be learned, visions yet seen. If you distinguish these people from others, you turn your back on yourself. You who know the way must lead the others. The truth is foggy to some, they don't share a clear vision. To this end, they become scattered, seeing with two sets of eyes.

They are one. You are one. I am one. Together we are one. Glorify it, embrace it, see it, understand it.

Different flowers blossom at different times. Every flower is beautiful in its own right. As I've said before, red is gray and yellow white. The differences are your own clouded perceptions.

The wizard, the pharaoh—each has its own method of magic, to all known. (Asmuth)

What was the purpose of Hitler's existence on the earth plane?

Death rears its head in many forms. A form of life. A soul so self-absorbed, in life death was an end. Does the end justify the means? A man so distraught, defiled his mother, believed in himself. A self-proclaimed leader, one to teach the masses in such a way. A legacy for all to see.

Tar and feathers would suit him fine, but what of those who were lost at the slashing sword. The knights, proud, proclaimed his death. Must we relive the dark ages—an age of distant terror. He (Hitler) spoke for many—those who mocked and defiled him.

Justice reigns in lieu of terror. Justice for the few. But the souls amassed for the cause can be held in memory. Memories are what keep us aligned with the truth. The truth shall reign. (Asmuth)

How can the survivors of the Holocaust and their descendants ease their pain?

Ovens of fire, screams of anguish and pain. Forsake those who betrayed you. Atrocities abound but to an end they came. Fear no more, the end draws near. An end to the bigotry and hatred, shared by all. No man, woman, or child shall escape the terror.

Martyrs of power. The death, the dying, marred in conspiracy. Who ever can forget the pain endured.

Coffins of terror, death without notice. Relive it or deny it—is this really a choice.

To the survivors I say, you will always remember the pain endured. Surviving is sometimes a fate worse than death. You who were left behind are a symbol to the callous display of anger. The pain is enormous, my heart pains for you.

Believe that for no other reason than mistrust and hate that these atrocities were brought upon you. Many lost their lives, their hopes, their dreams. But I say to all of you, live your dreams. Dreams spared, to be shared. (Shamani)

Where did AIDS come from?

The bridge across forever. The bridge is built on a foundation. A foundation of ideas—blatant mistrust of ideals.

The causes, the denials of the spirit. Cause and effect, who can say?

The red blood of a monkey, a laboratory, conceived by a few who saw righteousness in their cause. Injected into humanity, carve out the soul, misintentions. Lives to be spared but alas a canyon was created. A bigger thing than ever imagined. Could this be the end of humanity? (Shamani)

Why did AIDS begin with gay men?

A butte rises above the desert floor as a tribute to those who have passed before you. It is a monument to guide you along the path to the truth and light. Many of you have borne false testimony against each other. From a pebble to a boulder to a planet, the tale of AIDS has grown. The distant sky radiates blue, a symbol of hope for those afflicted with AIDS.

Where did it all begin, you ask? AIDS, as you know it, was conceived in a laboratory. Some would call it a laboratory of doom, while others would call it a laboratory of truth. Those who developed the AIDS virus viewed it as a way to perpetuate their conception of the truth. In "reality" (if it really exists), the truth was a reflection of their own insecurity and inadequacy. They conceived a weapon of doom to destroy what they did not understand in themselves. They felt if gay men were eliminated from the population, they would become stronger in their sexual identity. If the truth be known, they only became weaker.

Many of you have suffered by the actions of a few. But remember, all of you are responsible for perpetuating the prejudice associated with AIDS. It is up to each of you to recognize that your own feelings of insecurity and inadequacy fuel the spread of AIDS, and other illnesses and diseases. Do you really need to blame yourself or a specific group for the spread of AIDS? Remember that those who conceived of AIDS blamed "gay" men for their own insecurity and inadequacy.

Develop a clear vision of who you are and live by it. Be strong in your self-identity and sexual identity, but also respect others' rights to the same. If you dislike another person for the choices they make, look within and see your own reflection. You often criticize others for that which you do not like in yourself.

I ask you not to focus on the origin of AIDS. Instead, focus on that which unites all of us—love. Love yourself and each other, for in love you will discover who you truly are. (Shamani)

What would you say to someone who is homophobic?

Why do you deny your own sexuality? You mask your own inadequacy and insecurity through the fear of a group of individuals that you do not understand.

You ponder the concept of "homosexuality." You plaster it with labels—you can't see beyond yourself. Why do you deny another soul the right of free expression? You create models of decency and a code of ethics by which others should adhere to. What if the same models and codes were placed upon you—could you adhere to them?

The fear grows within you. It is like an unleashed rabid dog. Can you control it—the fear? Where does the foundation of your fear lie? Is it buried deep within you, do you have a childhood memory of abuse by a man or a woman?

The steps to recovery are often difficult. First, you must face the fear. Is it fair to blame an innocent person for that which lies within you? Do not let the self-abuse continue.

Face your fear with courage and determination. Replace the fear with love for yourself. Be secure with your own identity. For when you are secure with your own sexual identity, the light of your spirit will shine through to dissolve all your fears. (Asmuth)

Why did nuclear power evolve?

Nuclear power evolved out of a disease of the heart. Feelings of insecurity packed into a drum filled with powder. The powder shall rain down upon the whole earth.

Nuclear power also evolved out of a need to control others. If you are the only one who has nuclear power, then you make the rules. What happens when more than one has it—then you must increase what you have. So as you see, the goal of security becomes a game of insecurity.

Nuclear power was developed under the guise of an alternative energy source. There are those who see the true value of this as an alternative energy source. But, there are also those who are focused on death and destruction.

The fascination with nuclear power can be likened to your fascination with the sun. The sun is a million times more powerful. It provides all that you need for life on earth. Yet, too few of you harness its true energy.

The struggles of false power will continue until you learn the true potential of personal power. (Shamani)

Will we use nuclear power to help or destroy ourselves?

Are the branches of the tree filled with leaves or are they bare? I see weapons of mass destruction which were created by the "greatest minds" on earth. Earth will either live or die by these weapons. I ask you, why don't these "great minds" work to create a beneficial use for nuclear power? The weapons you create are filled with insecurity and inadequacy. Why not perpetuate life instead of death with nuclear power? The research has been done but it is misapplied. The conceptions of a few will have repercussions for many.

Creation or destruction? I foresee a time of decision approaching when the so-called leaders of your world will be forced to make a decision of eternal war or eternal peace on earth. There will be those who are bent on destruction and those who want peace. A line will be drawn between the two. The earth plane will be frozen in time.

But alas, the light shall radiate upon the earth and eternal peace shall reign. The consciousness of the earth and those on the earth shall be raised and changed forever. All shall know love and peace, war will be a myth of the past. However, the past shall be etched in the soul's memory. For we must never forget where we have come from. The ideas of the present are borne from the past.

Your future on earth seems uncertain and rightly so. Do not allow the truth to be hidden. Cast your doubts and fears aside and prepare yourself to be embraced in the light of the spirit.

Nuclear power will help you to see your true fate, but not before you are faced with imminent destruction. (Shamani)

Chapter 12:
Answers About Spirituality

Who is God, what is God, and where is God—these are questions many of you ask. You search your life looking for the answers to these immortal questions. When times are tough, who do you ask for? A god, in one form or another, someone or something to save you from illness, injury, or death. Who can save you from what you have freely chosen? Admonition of sin to a blank face, do you wait for a voice to tell you it's all right? Well, wait no longer. I am here to tell you it's all right. Though, you should be telling yourself. Who am I to tell you what you already know. The same is with God and spirituality.

The spirit rises in each of us, much like the rising sun. Some of us are asleep most of our life, while others are awake from the beginning. Which religion is right and which religion is wrong? No single religion on Earth can profess the entire truth, because the truth lies within each of us. What you don't realize is that the concept of different religions only serves to alienate you from one another. From one you were conceived, to one you shall return. So, why do you seek to separate yourselves through myths and fantasies, communicated over thousands of years? There is one single purpose in the universe, that is LOVE. So I say to you, love all people and all things equally, love them as you love yourself.

Whatever form your god takes, remember it is love that joins all of us. We are all one in love, is this not what your God professes?

You have many questions concerning religion and spirituality. I ask you, what is the difference between the two? Can you deny others the freedom to express themselves? One need not go to a church, synagogue, temple, or other place of worship in order to be saved. God, in whatever form you believe in, speaks to each and every one of you. There are no chosen people, only those you choose to put on a pedestal. There is so much you have yet to learn, but if you help each other, everyone will learn. Learn to love and respect each other.

Enlightenment is a gift, though it can not be bought. You must earn it by attaining knowledge and wisdom. So as you search for the answers to the immortal questions of your time, remember others have asked the same questions for thousands of years. Remember, the answers lie within each of us but until you ask the right questions, the answers will elude you.

I challenge you to ponder each question and answer in this chapter. If you do, you will truly discover your own spirituality and realize that we are all one. Take a trip, whether it be short or long, and discover the truth about your own spirituality. Remember we are all equal and together we are one. (Asmuth)

How can we find our own spirituality?

The warrior princess uses a shield to protect herself from her enemies. Are these enemies of truth? The blood and tears she has shed are for you. You are the shield and indeed you have protected yourself from the truth.

In order to find your own spirituality, you must first be willing to love yourself. For love of yourself must originate with you. You are the beacon of light that shines in the night for all to see.

You must come to know yourself—all parts of yourself—those parts you like and those you dislike. Only when you do this will you come to know who you really are. Seek to know the truth about yourself. Remember, the truth can wear many disguises, it is up to you to see beneath the disguise. When you know love, you will know the truth. This is the key to finding your own spirituality, a symbol of the truth.

So you ask, how can you as an individual do this? First of all, set aside a few minutes or a few hours each day to be with yourself. Think of how much of your time you give to others. And think of how much time you spend on "meaningless" routine tasks. (Everything has meaning and purpose, I only use the word "meaningless" to awaken your consciousness.) Find meaning and purpose in everything that you do. When I say take time to be with yourself, I mean quiet time. Relax your mind and body, lay still on a chair, in a bed, or on the grass. Let it be a place where you can meditate, pray, or think. Relax and go within the far reaches of your mind and focus on nothing but the here and now. Do not think about what has happened to you today. For today will soon be a memory for tomorrow.

Spirituality is an individual thing. Do not seek to find it in a book, church, monastery, synagogue, or temple. These things may help you to discover who you are but they will not give you spirituality. The spirit lies within you. Your soul is the foundation of love and truth. Now go within, and find and develop your own spirituality. You so richly deserve this and much more. If you should tire along the way, remember that love and truth shall shield and protect you from harm. (Shamani)

Can you talk about our need for organized religion?

To this I say, be true to yourself. Let no one else tell you what and who you should be. Let your conscience be your guide. The way to truth is different for everyone, no two roads are the same.

The answers are different for everyone. There is no one single truth—if there were, we would all be the same.

I see wars fought over this idea of religion. Bloodshed for whom, for what reason. Man against man, woman against woman, child against child. Weapons of mass destruction, built to wage war over differences in ideas. For what reason? Are we all not of the same spirit?

Your need for organized religion seems to be rooted in isolation. The Eskimo who stands alone in the cold will freeze to death. So, he or she seeks the comfort of another and so on. Together, you build things, the foundation of civilization was built on this principle. Just as you and I work together, sharing ideas—others do the same. We all need to feel a sense of belonging. Through our interactions, we feel this.

In ancient Egypt, monuments were built for the Gods. In this, people gathered and felt a sense of purpose. The pharaohs were lavished with gold and gems. (Asmuth)

How can we know if our spiritual leaders' words are true?

The clouds often seem gray when they are truly white. Perception is the key to unlocking the truth. Only those who profess the truth can deny the truth. False prophets may come and go but only those whose words have stood the test of time can be those of the truth.

The truth can be disguised in many ways. Many can tell you what they believe the truth is, but is that the truth? Remember that you are a symbol of the truth and the light. Can what others tell you stand in the light or does it wither away in darkness? What does your intuition tell you, to believe or disbelieve? The truth can be twisted and distorted to fit into any belief system. Just think of your various religions and political groups. I do not mock any of these, I only call them to your attention to illuminate the truth.

The truth can be anything you want it to be. You can serve it or it can serve you. Your spiritual leaders on the earth plane, for the most part believe in themselves. By believing in themselves, they also believe that what they profess is the truth.

Again, I say it is up to you to decide what fits into your belief system. Remember, the truth is based on love, a love of all things, living and non-living. The truth encompasses all that is, was, and ever will be. If anyone tells you otherwise, then they undeniably do not speak of the truth. If you can see the truth clearly without obstruction, then clearly you see the truth. (Asmuth)

What do you think about televangelists?

Ministers for truth or ministers for money—you decide. Do they speak of ancient myth or legend? Myths are based on half-truth while legends are often based on truth. They look to words for truth, they do not realize that the words come from them.

They believe in themselves though the truth often becomes contorted.

They speak of demons, condemning those who do not believe. They create fear in the innocent. The creation of fear in the masses can be very "powerful." The false power they (televangelists) wield allows them to remain separate from the masses. They feel they are the chosen ones to speak to God. (Remember all souls are equal, all are chosen to stand in the light.)

The fears of many are provoked into verse. The verse becomes the truth and the truth becomes the law. Lawless minds reach out to touch the fabric of their being. But often, the people (who follow the "law") find that they are separated from themselves. The truth should unite people, not separate them.

And so I say without reservation, the land the televangelists promise may not be the promised land. Make a promise to yourself that you will always seek the truth. Remember the truth lies within your soul, be true to yourself. (Asmuth)

Why do humans have a need for a god-figure?

For the same reasons that you need me. You need someone, some thing, or some entity to guide you along your life path. Belief in a higher intelligence has and always will be prevalent in the universe. As your soul evolves, its purpose becomes more well-defined. It aspires to reach new levels of awareness by attaining higher levels of consciousness. Your soul's goal is to become one with "the essence of one."

Whether you believe in a god-figure is not important. What is important is that you believe in yourself. For if you believe in yourself, you will see the god-figure that you have created is alive and well in your soul.

Most often, your need for a god-figure stems from the need to believe in something outside of yourself. A god-figure is a control mechanism by which you can gauge your soul's growth.

A god-figure can also be manipulated and molded into something or someone to blame or praise. The truth is, many of you need a god-figure to guide you along your life path. One day you may meet the vision of the god-figure you have created. If you do, you will realize that the god-figure was a part of you all the time. Only now, you have come to believe in yourself and you are "the essence of one." (Shamani)

Can you talk about Jesus a bit? Did he exist?

Jesus, a man with purpose. He came to you with a vision, a vision so clear, to share what he had learned. Conceived of the spirit, a symbol of truth and justice, a symbol of good.

Jesus took a form for all to see, all to remember. A glowing white light, pure energy, pure light.

Jesus existed just as you and I. Do we question our own existence?

Jesus, neither man nor woman. Though his appearance was male-like, only to convince them of his presence. The days when he appeared were filled with discontent, dissatisfaction, disillusion, and disenchantment. So he rang a bell for all to hear—a bell of peace and love.

Jesus, the embodiment of truth—truth to stand the test of time. The spirit of truth lives on.

Look up at the stars, see the light, the brilliance. In it, you shall see Jesus.

Jesus, Gandhi, Allah—born of the same light but took different forms. All these exist in the minds of those who believe. We are born with beliefs, beliefs of distant places and times. Rehearsals of the mind. Our mind is ever so powerful—born of the spirit, in the spirit, by the spirit. Let no one take that away. (Asmuth)

Could you tell us about Jesus' life on earth?

Stars of gold shone down upon the earth, conceived in the light of the spirit. Oh spirited one, sent to teach expression of our souls, expressions of love. For love is the center of all things. Things are just things. Until love is introduced, these things have no meaning. The meaning of life is embodied in love. Love is a true feeling, an expression of all that is. This was the embodiment of Jesus.

Born of the spirit, but never died? Do we die? No, we are only reborn. Death is a myth, a trick of the hand. But it does give us an end, a measure of where we are. It exists in our minds to teach us. With finality comes rebirth, rebirth into new ideas. Ideas whose time has come, revealed to us in many ways, divinely inspired.

Seek the truth as Jesus did and you will find happiness. (Asmuth)

What can we learn from Jesus?

As I have said, seek the truth. Within the truth lies all that is good and right. Don't waste your time with half-truths and lies. This is fiction and fantasy. These are true in their own right but neither can stand the test of time. If you allow yourself to be led down this road, you will find you must turn yourself around. Else, you shall go round and round and round. Circular motion, good for the planets (orbiting the sun), but not good for you. You are the director of your life, I am only here to guide you and help you. A role I enjoy immensely—it gives me great pleasure. I am glad to hear that you are listening. Your actions speak highly of you.

You are on the right path and if you should stray, I will put you back on the path. Pure essence, pure love awaits you. (Asmuth)

What was Jesus' life purpose?

Remember that a baby's crib should be built to withstand a thousand earthquakes. The foundation on which your beliefs and ideas are built should be strong and able to withstand intense scrutiny. The scrutiny of a thousand souls bearing down on one soul. Should a monument of truth be built to this one soul? There are many of you who deserve such monuments. But how many people do you know that would build a monument or statue in your honor?

So what Jesus teaches you is to build a monument of truth to yourself. It is all well and good to honor "his" physical presence but do not forget what he came to the earth plane to do. Jesus' life purpose was twofold. Are there not two sides to everything? Oh indeed there is, and this is what Jesus came to the earth plane to teach you. To love and be loved, to give love and share love—a very simple concept. But a concept which many of you have yet to learn. Love must be unconditional, for conditional love only creates barriers between you and others.

The whispers of the wind unite each of you. Can each of you attest to this? Do you listen to the wind or do you keep a deaf ear to it?

Jesus, Mohammed, Buddha, and other spiritual leaders of many are one in the same. Your perception is the only difference between them. The foundation of their beliefs is the same, only the words they speak are for the benefit of each group of peoples. If you sit down and compare what each of them says, you will see that their voices and words blend together.

So you see, Jesus' life was and still is a testament to life, light, and truth. Without these three things, life would not be possible. For in life, you seek the light and truth. In the light, you seek life and the truth. And in truth, you seek life and the light. Jesus showed you that you are the embodiment of all three, from three you shall become one. For one is the true essence of your being. Seek to become one and one you shall become.

Remember the pyramids have three corners and three sides which rise to unite as one. Bring the three parts of yourself together—mind, body, and spirit—and unite as one. For when you have achieved this, you will see Jesus' life purpose illuminated clearly within you. For you will be one with the essence of Jesus. (Shamani)

What can we learn from the Bible?

Ah, a question of fact or fiction. The truth takes many shapes and sizes. There is truth in the Bible, but there is also judgment.

The Bible is a book which has served as a guide to life for many on Earth. Many believe wholeheartedly in the words contained in its pages. Thoughts transcribed eons ago and duplicated on the crudest form of paper. The truth became an inspiration for many to see and hear. But there came a time when those who sought power over the communion of words sought to change the words. These people in their own righteous minds developed a code of ethics which they thought other people should live by. And so they interpreted the words of inspiration into their own book of truth.

The truth is that which can stand in the light. Can the Bible in its many different forms, interpretations, and translations stand completely in the light?

The Bible is based on truth but what is on its pages is not necessarily the truth. As you can see, the interpretations of the words in this book have led to endless wars, both present and past. How can such a book of "truth" divide people?

The Bible teaches you this and much more. It also teaches you that if you give power to one thing as the sole source of truth, then you are truly blind to the truth. (Shamani)

What is heaven?

Heaven on earth, a destined place of perfection. A place we call home for our soul. A final resting-place. It means so many things to so many people.

Angels of mercy brought down to a land of eternal bliss. Rose gardens, gardens of joy. The joy radiates within and outward.

Pure love of the heart. Love is at the heart of all that is. Heaven is that place where love resides. Think of life without love and there would be no heaven.

Heaven is neither a place in space or time, it just is. Circles of light and ecstasy in the purest of forms. Where is heaven, you ask? Look up and see the stars, the stars shine brightly upon you.

Heaven is personless, shapeless, without form. As I said, heaven is a place to call home. Heavenly souls, souls guided, come home and see the place I call heaven (your home). (Asmuth)

Is there a hell?

Hell is a manifestation of the mind. Again, if you believe such a place with demon and devil spirits exists, and feel that you deserve it, then you can put yourself there. It's a sort of self-imposed hell.

Why would you choose such a place for yourself? It's like choosing death over life or hate over love. Those of you who are on a path of self-destruction experience this idea of hell. I speak of those who are alcoholics, drug addicts, abusers, and abusees. All of this is self-destructive behavior. Why not choose self-love?

Hell is what you make it. If you create a conception of it, then you can live in it. But for me, it seems such a waste of life.

Embrace the love and be guided by it. (Asmuth)

What is Armageddon? Will Armageddon occur?

Armageddon is a manifestation of your mind. Throughout time (as you conceive it), many have heralded the end of the earth. Indeed, you are reaching a time on earth where all eyes are focused. The thoughts and energies of many earth-bound souls are focused on the coming millennium. It is a time of change.

Old ideas, ideas that have not benefited the many, will be tested. The consciousness on the earth plane is changing rapidly. Many of you are accelerating both mentally and spiritually.

There will be divisions, in fact a great division among souls. There will be those who believe in the vision of truth and those who will choose to remain in the darkness.

I see a major shift in the collective spirit on earth. The path of love and truth will be well-lighted. In order to find the path, each individual will have to find the light within and be guided by it.

There will be many bridges. The bridges of faith will be tested. Many people will see that the ideas of the past have not worked. Greed, jealousy, selfishness, perversity, dishonesty, hate, bias, prejudice, and deception will be cast aside. All who cling to these will not be able to weather the journey. All will be called to embrace the light and love.

Some will view this as Armageddon, the end of the world. With each ending, there is a new beginning.

Set a course for yourself and align yourself with all that is good and positive. The pot of gold awaits those who persevere. (Shamani)

Why do some people believe in demons and devils? And do they exist?

Demons and devils, creations of the mind. Are the stars in the sky real? Yes, in your mind. If you acknowledge that something exists, then it does. Often, we want to create things outside of ourselves. We are not content with ourselves and therefore create images of gods to worship. For some, it is their wish to go beyond the worldly realm and contact spirits. When the mind is opened by alternative methods (drugs, alcohol, malicious intentions), there lies a dark side. When you choose love, you bask in the light. This is what I choose. Some spirits choose to dwell in the darkness. Darkness is oblivion.

If you open yourself to these spirits, they will take many disguises, often masked in love to deceive you. If you stay in the light, you are well protected.

You are ultimately in control of your mind. Unless you acknowledge or create these so-called demon or devil spirits, then you have nothing to fear. Nothing and no one can control you, unless you allow them. Remain focused and at one. (Asmuth)

Is there a God, god?

God is within each of us. Pure essence without a trace. Religions of your world ask this age-old question. Who do they worship, the masses congregating in a place? They want to see all that is. Life without light, life without God. Even in the darkest of places, there is still light.

The rocking chair of faith goes back and forth, swaying in the wind. In search of wisdom, eternal all-powerful truth. Where is it?

For centuries people have searched high and low for Gods. People worship many things and people as gods. If we reach God, do you find true happiness? Gods, things to put on our shelves. When we don't need them anymore, we throw them away.

Magic was once thought to be from the gods, those who used it were gods. But the gods perished and so did the magic. So I say to you, revere no one and no thing as a god. The spirit lies within, go seek it and you shall find God. (Asmuth)

What is enlightenment?

Enlightenment is a level of understanding by which all things are viewed with love. Loving oneself is a level of enlightenment. If you can look beyond yourself and see the need to help others, then you have attained a certain level of enlightenment.

Enlightenment can not be bought or sold, it can only be shared. You who are enlightened have a gift, a gift which you can choose to share with others. You may not be enlightened in all areas of your life. This should not worry you, for there is much you have yet to learn. Enlightenment is neither patient nor impatient. So have patience with yourself and realize that enlightenment comes to those who are ready to embrace it, yet do not seek it.

Am I enlightened, you might ask? Well, if the truth be known, I am exactly where I need to be. If that means I am enlightened, then label me as such. When you have reached a level of enlightenment, you will surely find that there is no need for labels. For you know who you are! (Asmuth)

How do we find the path to enlightenment?

Oh symbol of light, lead me down the path. The path is long and arduous, but you are up to the task. Do you wish to find the light at the end of the tunnel? The tunnel may seem endless but I am with you every step of the way. Every step of the way, the eagle and the wolf walk with you. The eagle is your spirit rising above you, the wolf is your protector. The wolf is a symbol of your walking on the earth. In both, you can seek the answers, a fine line to walk.

Enlightenment is not just a word, it can be as abstract as you or I. It is not a place or a thing—it has no dimensions.

Light the way to yourself, peace of mind, contentment—this is enlightenment. Abstract concepts I grant you.

The church, the stained glass windows let some of the light in. The masses join to become enlightened. What they seek is outside of them, they think. Place a belief outside yourself.

Think about this, who am I? I am a being of light, ever glowing, ever present. How do I reach the road to enlightenment? There is no road, only paths that lead you there. There or here—so abstract. Do you know where there or here is? It is the same as enlightenment. It just is. So I say to you, take a moment, make your mind blank, go within, and just be. (Shamani)

Chapter 13:
Answers From Beyond

Many of you may ask, what lies beyond the earth plane? Look at your reflection in a window, you will see your past, present, and future. Come to the Garden of Eden, but do not bring any baggage. For when you incarnate onto the earth plane and when you leave the earth plane, you only have your soul. You carry your soul and your soul carries you, it is that simple. Magical and mystical to some and agonizing and fearful to others.

How you prepare your soul to make the transition to the earth plane and beyond is your responsibility. Sure, there are those (your guardian angels, spirit guides, or those who watch over you) who will guide and protect you before, during, and after the transition. But, ultimately it is you who must make the transition. From birth to death and death to birth, to many of you death is viewed as an end to your life. But I tell you, it is only the beginning.

Find the magic within your soul, the magic will take you way beyond yourself to a place of light and truth. A place where all things are possible, dreams come true, and fantasy merges with reality. A place undeniably referred to as "the essence of one." Are you ready, and is your soul ready, to embrace "the essence of one"?

Create a vision of love, peace, and harmony in your mind, let it flow through your body, and let it merge with your spirit. Now your mind, body, and spirit are one. Take this feeling of oneness and embark on a reading journey through this chapter. All of what you read you may not understand, but I ask you to open your mind, body, and spirit to new thoughts and ideas. You may find yourself reading this chapter over and over. Keep in mind that all the information we give you is for your higher good.

Whether you are at the beginning or end of your life on the earth plane, remember it is life not death which propels you forward. Prepare for life now, do not wait until death to make amends with those you love, including yourself.

Life and death, death and life—where did it all begin and when will it all end? The answers to these questions can be found in the pages that follow, but the awareness that comes from knowing the answers lies within you. I invite you to open your mind and prepare to receive the answers to the immortal questions of life. (Asmuth)

Where did all life begin, including yours?

Ah, one of the greatest secrets of the universe. Where all life began did not exist before all life began, it is not a place that can be defined through your conventional form of communication—your language. Where life began is as abstract and puzzling as life itself.

You ask where "one" came from. Many of us ponder this same question. Until you return to the essence of one, that which is perfect love, we will not know the origin of one. All I can tell you is that one "is." "Is" is a state of being which can not be described or defined.

As you elevate your soul to higher levels of consciousness, the answer to this question will become clearer. You must step out of your mind. Think of being in a dream and going several levels beyond the dream. Where would you be? Could you define where you are? The answer you seek has no answer, it just "is."

Remember that all thoughts and energies are one. From one you were conceived, to one you shall return. One is all that is, has been, and ever will be. Once you accept this one truth, you will begin to understand where all life began. My life began where yours did, we are all one. If you need to know from where I came, beyond the one, to this I say, I was conceived on a plane of blue. The blue surrounds me, my thoughts and energy radiate in blue. I am the essence of blue.

Most often you seek more definitive and concrete answers to your questions. But the universe is not concrete, it is abstract and defies definition. If you learn to open your mind, you will see that there are no limits to your understanding. Remember that the earth plane is very much a physical space. However, do not limit yourself to the physical world.

Go within and "touch" your soul, you will see what I say. Then you can tell me what you see. Life has no beginning and end, it just "is." (Shamani)

How do we choose our birthplace and our birth parents?

Radiant light beams down upon you.

Have I been here before and have I met you? These are questions you often ask. To everything, there is a higher purpose. You have choices. You made choices before incarnating into your present life.

We often choose places that are familiar to us. Our birth parents may be friends, siblings, parents, sons, or daughters from a previous life. There is no set pattern which I can describe. It is all a matter of choices intertwined with your lessons. There are no chance meetings or acquaintances.

This is a life you have chosen. Many times, you may question your existence as well as your choices. But I say to you, there is a lesson in everything you do. There is order in everything. One day you will clearly see the rhyme and reason for everything. Until then, trust the universe. The universe will provide everything you need. (Shamani)

A tree has many branches. All of the branches extend from the stem/the trunk. We all grow at different rates and in different directions. Before you are born into this life, you are given choices much like the branches. Many options lie before you, what is it that you come to this life to learn? Where and with whom can your lessons best be learned? Will there be pain, will there be joy, will there be honesty, will there be dishonesty, will there be love, will there be hate? All of these questions enter your mind.

You see scenarios of your life choices played out in your mind. You know what lessons of positive growth await you.

There will be windy and cold days and bright and sunny days. In each day, there will be opportunities for growth. You may not like them but they stand firm, waiting for you to embrace them. You may slide back or move forward quickly.

Each soul sacrifices for another, this is out of love not dependence. But many times, you can not see any purpose why you were born. You scorn the ground you walk on, you question life in its entirety. You think of taking your own life prematurely. We tend to repeat lessons we have not learned. Just as you, I have lessons of positive growth.

Lessons of positive growth await you, embrace them with love. (Asmuth)

Do we choose the time of our birth and our death?

Does the time of your birth and your death fascinate you? These are "moments" during which you make the transition from/to birth and death. Think of yourself as a time traveler and you choose the time of arrival and departure. While on the earth plane, you are not conscious of your birth and death. These are times when your unconscious mind takes over. You are led through a tunnel of light, a tunnel you have traveled many times before.

The time of your birth and your death are not random events of nature, as so many of you believe. Your birth and your death on the earth plane are necessary in terms of your higher purpose. Your soul's higher purpose is first and foremost in any decision you make.

Let me say that your birth and your death are both beginnings. I ask you not to see death as the end of everything you know. It is a new beginning, it is life after life on the earth plane. You have so much in birth and you have so much in death. There are millions of souls who have made the transition from birth to death and death to birth. It is not difficult once you have done it a few times. When the time comes for you to make the transition again, you will remember. We (your guardian angels, spirit guides, or those who watch over you) will be there to greet you.

Before you incarnate onto the earth plane, your soul is given many choices for your higher learning and purpose. Think of it as seeing a movie about your life played before your eyes. You see the choices for your birth, your death, and your life in between. Remember time is your perception on the earth plane. In essence, you can not choose time because time is not fixed. All the events of your life will seemingly unfold according to a time sequence. This is only for your understanding and so that you can create order in your life.

The colors of the rainbow are brightly illuminated before you. If you try to find the beginning or end of the rainbow, you will find it is ever elusive. The same is with you, your life has no beginning or end. The same is with time, it has no beginning or end. Yet you and time are seen by many to exist. They exist in your mind and for your mind. Remember how you spend your "time" on the earth plane is as important as the "time" you choose to arrive on and depart from it. Let your life be symbolic of a spectacular colorful rainbow, one which will be a model for others to live by. (Shamani)

How do souls begin the incarnation process?

Like a star first born, a spark, then a slight glow, then a radiant burst of light. A light so bright, all who look at it are blinded. Then the light recedes.

A dark space where many souls are gathered, the doors open, and a great bright light shines upon you. Seven guides, predisposed with the knowledge required for you to pursue your life path. This information is shared with you. You are given guidance and many choices for your life path. You choose what you feel is best for you in the light of the spirit. You have choices, the choices are freedom. No judgment, no retribution—the choices are completely out of love. For through love can the truth only be sought.

You are led down a long hallway to a room where you can see all your choices played out visually. You again make your choices but everything must stand true in the light of the spirit. You are given the keys to unlock this incarnation and then into it you are born. The rest is up to you. As I said before, we are here to guide you and help you along the path. The path of self-love or self-destruction—make your choices wisely. Wisdom comes through truth—always be true to yourself. Do not let others sway you. You have the potential to do good, why waste it? Live a life of truth—the rewards await you. (Asmuth)

Where do souls go after death?

Oh those souls who depart the earth plane. What is your personal conception of death? Is it the end-all or just the beginning of a new journey? Light or darkness, what is your choice? Do your beliefs stand in the light of the truth? The truth about death is unbeknownst to many. Many fear it, few approach it with open arms and dignity.

I ask you to align yourself with the light of the spirit. The spirit shall appear to you before you pass over. You will be given a choice, it is up to you to decide your fate. You are the ruler of your destiny. Make your choices wisely in life and at your time of departing from the earth plane, you will not fear death.

Death is a manifestation of your mind. It is a way for you to measure your life's accomplishments. I am not here to judge your accomplishments.

You were born from the spirit, to the spirit you shall return. There is life after life (on the earth plane). It is up to you to embrace the love inside of you. For in love, you shall find renewed life. Paradise awaits those who believe it exists. No one is denied entry into the light of the spirit, but your soul must make the choice.

Those who do not make a choice are encouraged by their guardian angels or spirit guides to pass over. In order for the transition to be complete, your soul must embrace the love and the light. The light shines within each of us, and to the light we must return. For in the light, there is eternal life. (Asmuth)

How many souls are there? Did we all come from the beginning, or do new souls manifest?

There are an infinite number of souls. There are many souls which exist beyond the earth plane. Remember that the universe is limitless and forever expanding with each new thought and idea. There is so much you have yet to discover. There are no limits to what you can discover, only the limits of your mind.

I have spoken previously of the concept of oneness and its importance. One is all that is, has been, and ever will be. All souls are one. All thoughts, ideas, and energy forms are one. Think of all/everything, that is one. One is perfection. Love is the essence of one. You can not see, feel, hear, or taste one, for one just "is." One is not a state of being. Your soul knows one, for it is one.

You have all come from one. One is the beginning, the end, and all things in between. Indeed, new souls manifest from new energies, the energies of thoughts and feelings. But remember that the new souls are part of one.

You/your soul has been conceived from one, to one you shall return. (Asmuth)

Do some souls choose to bypass the earth plane?

For every thought or idea, there is an equal thought or idea. This is known as the relationship of thoughts and ideas, kindred spirits unite for your understanding. You have a relationship with yourself. The relationship is based on a commitment to seek the truth. This is your soul's primary purpose. For through the truth, you discover love. Love helps you to grow, no matter where you are, whether on or beyond the earth plane.

So you ask, do some souls bypass the earth plane? To this I say yes, and as I have said, your soul is committed to seeking the truth. The earth plane is one of many planes. Your soul has the choice whether to enter or bypass the earth plane or any other plane. But remember, the choice must always be for your soul's higher purpose, that which is the truth.

All of your soul's lessons lie on the earth plane or beyond (on another plane). Remember that there are several levels of consciousness on each plane. Each level of consciousness equates with a level of developed knowledge, understanding, and wisdom.

A soul may choose to bypass or re-enter the earth plane. If a soul has reached the highest level, it may choose to enter another plane or re-enter the earth plane to help other souls with their lessons. If a soul is not ready to enter the earth plane, it may bypass the earth plane. Some souls re-enter the earth plane immediately, while others wait.

Knowledge and wisdom can be attained on any level of any plane. The key is to aspire to the highest level of consciousness. For in higher consciousness, you will "see" the truth. (Shamani)

Why do some souls incarnate for a short time—for example, babies who die before their first year?

The shortness of breath cannot be measured in time. A baby's breath—a subtle expression of life. Is your life predestined? The lessons you (your soul) must learn cannot be measured in time. Your soul has the choice of life on the earth plane. You see all of your life as it will happen. For some souls, the lessons are quick.

For those on the earth plane, it is difficult to understand the death of a baby or a child. Life on earth is seemingly uncertain. But if you knew when you would "die," would you live your life differently? The eternal surprise awaits you—do not fear death. Death is but a transition into life. Embrace every moment, for in every moment is where the truth lies. (Asmuth)

Please talk about karma and how it works in the universe.

Is it better to give than to receive? Only if you remember that what you give will come back to you. This is the universal law of karma. It is a cycle based on a simple truth. There are no accidents or coincidences, just karma.

Karma is neither good nor bad, it just "is." If you can learn to work with the karma you have been given/chosen, your life will not seem like a merry-go-round. By this I mean, do you often go round and round in circles only to find yourself back where you started? Haven't you seen this movie many times, you should know the ending by now. If you know a plane is going to crash before you get on it, then why go on it? All of this simply asks, why do you feel the need to repeat your life lessons over and over?

Your present life is the summation of all past experiences, including those of your past lives. You come into this life holding all the knowledge and wisdom of the past. You can choose to ignore what you have learned or build upon what you have learned. If you give love, then you shall receive love. The choice seems easy, doesn't it?

There is individual and collective karma. Individual karma is that which every being inherits upon conception. Every thought and feeling you have contributes to your karma. Karma is simply your individual soul's lessons. Collective karma is the summation of all individual karmas. Each of you has a responsibility to each other for you are all one, we are all one. In terms of your world (the earth plane), there exists a collective earth karma. You are a major part of the earth's karma. You are part of the earth and the earth is part of you. If you care for and protect the earth, then the earth will care for and protect you. The same can be said if you do the opposite. Do you see how karma works now?

So I say, karma can be as easy or as difficult as you choose. The choices are always yours. Karma is a choice, plain and simple. What you do with it will determine your life on the earth plane and beyond. (Asmuth)

When do we stop incarnating?

You might as well ask, when do you stop growing? Each of your incarnations equates with a level of growth. Growth can be difficult or easy, depending on how readily you accept your lessons. Do you prefer to be spoon-fed or do you feed yourself? Each of your lessons is a challenge. You do not need to overcome or succumb to your lessons. When you are one with your lesson, then you have truly learned it.

From the point of your soul's conception, each of you who read this has had numerous incarnations. It is really not important to focus on how many incarnations you have had. Let it suffice that your presence on the earth plane is a testimony to your many incarnations. The earth plane is a level of consciousness which allows you to balance your karma. The earth plane is an accelerated learning ground. The earth itself is a symbol of balance. You can recognize much from the earth, recognize and understand the various cycles it endures while still remaining in balance. The cycles can be catastrophic or stable, yet there is always balance. So the same should be with you.

Once you have learned all the lessons you need to learn on the earth plane, you will rise to a new level of consciousness. On this level, you will continue to incarnate as many times as is necessary for your growth. You will continue to ascend to various levels. Eventually, you will unite with all that "is"—the essence of "one." When you are "one," you will "realize" that you are part of everything. You will be incarnation, growth, and lessons. You will know all that is, you shall be the truth and the light. So you ask, when do we stop incarnating? When we become the essence of all that is incarnation, devoid of words, description, form, or shape. (Asmuth)

Why do most of us live and die without knowledge of the other world? Why are some of us given the knowledge?

Knowledge of the "other world," that which lies beyond the earth plane, is etched in your soul's memory. As I have stated previously, when you are born (into your present life) and up to about three years, you have memory of the other world. The knowledge of it in the early stages of your life helps you to make the transition from the other world to the earth plane. The past and future is not as important as the present. The way you live your life is both a reflection of your past and future. This is a simple truth which I give you, but it is truly all the knowledge you need.

Many of you do not realize all that you are now is a summation of all that you have been and will be. You have knowledge of the other world, but you do not open your mind, body, and spirit to it. Some of you recognize these simple truths and apply them to your life paths. Each one of you is privileged in your own individual way. Each of you chooses your own life path.

Remember, you have all the knowledge you need. Believe in yourself, you are the ruler of your destiny. The beauty of one flower (your life) fills the hearts of many. The lilies of the valley line the path to knowledge and wisdom. It is up to you to align yourself with the path. When you are truly on the path, you will see that the knowledge of the "other world" is the knowledge that lies within you. They are one in the same. (Asmuth)

Why do some people go to the light and return—have near-death experiences?

Some of you have witnessed what it feels like to stand in the light, while on the earth plane. All of you who have gone to the light and returned feel a renewed sense of hope and love. You saw an image of yourself bathed in a bright white radiant light. I dare to say that the light you saw was that which radiates from you. For you who have returned to live another day on the earth plane, there is much I can say to you. The "near-death experience" is real. I do not say "was real" because "was" is "is." You experienced just a glimmer of all that "is"—the essence of love. Now that you have returned, you must fulfill your soul's purpose. In the light, you saw your soul's purpose brightly illuminated. Now, you have another chance to fulfill that purpose. So, place yourself in the light of yourself and feel a sense of renewed love. Love and light always surrounds you.

For those of you who wonder why some people have had near-death experiences, the answer is simple—divine intervention. When a soul is careening through the universe on a course of self-destruction, there are those of us who watch over you who become concerned with your life choices. You may think that you are moving along on the path of growth and learning. You may well be, but there is a higher purpose for your soul which you do not readily see. So we bring you to the light in hopes of illuminating your life to you, the life you have previously chosen before this incarnation. You have the choice to stay in the light or return. But remember it is your soul's choice, not necessarily your conscious mind's choice. Strange as this may seem, you know it is true. For the truth stands in the light. When it is "your time," you will go the light and become a beacon of light for all to see. The beacon of light will be the love that radiates from you. We (your spirit guides, guardian angels, or those who watch over you) will be there to receive you into the light of your soul. Until then, know that we are with you always. (Asmuth)

Can you tell us about angels?

The sirens of love blare for all to hear. Angels are what many of you call us. It is not important what you call us, only that you acknowledge our presence.

Angels are spirits like myself who come to the earth plane to protect and guide you. We have your life plan in hand—we know all that is and all that will ever be. As keepers of the knowledge, we have the responsibility to share it with you. But your soul must be open to receive it. Your mind and body must be in line with your soul.

It is important to keep your mind and body free of poisons or contaminants. By this I mean mind-altering substances. Much of what many of you eat is not for nourishment. Learn to nourish the body, mind, and soul with good thoughts and food. Take a natural approach, discover the magic of nature. Good health awaits those who will embrace it. Affirm your life on earth. We tell you these things with good intentions. Align yourself and open your mind, body, and spirit beyond the earth plane. Then you shall see and hear your angels.

The angels of love watch over you. Know that we are with you every moment of the day.

Many of you think of us as cherubs. We can take any form, whether physical or pure energy. We appear to you in a form that you are comfortable with. We embody love in its purest form. We are beings of the light.

One day we shall meet, whether it be on the earth plane or upon passing over. Remember that your angels are with you always, they truly love you. (Asmuth)

How many guides do we each have?

Let me first say that when I speak of guides, I refer to spirit guides, guardian angels, and those who watch over you. In any language, it means the same thing. Do not be offended by the amount of guides that you have. Think of your guides as spiritual advisers and counselors. Though you may not readily see us, we are always with you. We do not cast judgments, unless it is for your understanding of your higher purpose. It is only for your understanding, take no offense or defense.

The amount of guides that each of you have is variable. There are no set numbers/amounts that each of you have. It depends on the complexity of the lessons that you have chosen before entering the earth plane. None of your guides are strangers to you. Past lives and memories would surely reacquaint you, if you had access to such memories. Indeed you do have access, but first you must elevate your level of consciousness.

As a young child, you have many guides around you. This is a stage of uncertainty and you are perplexed by the life process. It is in this stage that you are most receptive to us physically and verbally. You often speak of us as "imaginary" playmates that only you can see. Alas, the winds of time whisk the memory of us away until you are ready to see us again.

Your guides may take many forms and shapes. They may appear as animals, plants, humans, or a concentrated form of light energy. Your guides are not limited to these forms, only by your thoughts or ideas of what they should be. Let it suffice to say that you will never be alone, there will always be at least one guide around you. Even as you transit between the earth plane and beyond in "death," you may feel that you are alone. But if you reach out and call for us, you will "feel" our hands reaching out to you and gently raising you toward the light and truth. All of us guides have been united in love, may you come to know the oneness we share with you. (Shamani)

Can you explain to us what our guides do for us throughout our lives?

We are your teachers, those who guide and protect you throughout your life from the beginning of conception. By the beginning of conception, I refer to your first incarnation from the essence of all that is. You have been guided toward the light. The light is the truth and love and all that is. Your spirit (soul) was given the choice to expand, to learn all that is.

And so, throughout your "life," you have existed on many planes. The earth plane is just one of these. The earth plane can be likened to a school of accelerated learning. There are many options available to you. There are many shapes and forms you can take. Those who read this have taken a human form. The human form is simple in nature and requires little to physically sustain it. The physical human form allows free expression of the soul.

Your mind has developed over eons. Much of the time, your mind is like a carousel. It just goes round and round and you seem to go nowhere. That is where your guides come in. Our purpose is to help you and guide you through the maze, which you call life on earth. We help you to make the decisions that are aligned with your higher purpose. Oftentimes, you shut us out of your consciousness.

When you are a child, we are working with you on a daily basis from the day you are born up to about age three. This is a time in which you are very receptive to us. You can see us and hear us. You often speak to us. During this time, we try to prepare you for your life's lessons. You are shown the power of love and healing through love. It is often a fun time for us because you truly and freely communicate with us.

After the age of about three years, you become bombarded with others' preconceptions of life. Your spirit (soul) starts to recede as if into a shell. Much of what you have seen on your own (as in seeing and talking to us) is challenged. Then your experiences with us become repressed memories.

As you develop through childhood, adolescence, and adulthood, we are always with you, watching over you. In your deepest and darkest moments when you feel all alone, we are beside you. Our arms reach out to hug you. The love we have for you cannot be measured in human terms. Love can only be measured in the terms you place on it. We ask you to open yourselves, either through prayer, meditation, or silent thought. You must raise your consciousness to see and talk to us. We await your presence.

Life is an affirmation. We are here to help you affirm your own life. You have freely chosen your life. But remember always that you are not alone. Recount one time in your life when you may have died at the hands of yourself or another, but you lived. In that moment, we were there to catch you and restore you to life. We pulled you up so that you could affirm life once again.

The love we feel for you can only be described in a rainbow of colors which surround you. The tears we shed are tears of joy for you. You are each a true expression of "God's beauty."

Know that you are always protected in the light. For in the light, there is oneness. Let your spirit soar to new heights. Embrace the love, embrace each other. (Asmuth)

How can we find our way to the light, the truth?

When you can pass through the stars in the universe, then you will truly be one. When you are one, you will know the light and truth. You will be the light and truth.

In order to find the way to the light and truth, you must first believe that the light and truth exist. If you believe in yourself, then you have laid the foundation. All that you do, think, and feel must be able to stand in the light. In other words, you must be honest with yourself and others. You also must love yourself and others.

The light and truth always shine upon you, though you may shield your eyes from it. Many of you are afraid of what you might see, for the light penetrates all disguises of falsity.

Think of a divining rod, used to find sources of water beneath the earth's surface. The divining rod works on the principles of magnetics (magnetic energy). The divining rod aligns with the magnetic field of the subsurface body (object). Use this principle to find your way to the light and truth. Align yourself with all that is love. Through love you will know the light and the truth.

Love is more than a verbal and physical expression. True love is the alignment of your mind, body, and spirit in the light.

For many of you who read this, the concepts of truth and light are not entirely clear to you. I have opened a whole new world of truth to you. I ask you to elevate your level of consciousness, open your mind, cast out the doubts and fears, and embrace love. Most importantly, do these things at your own pace but remain focused. If you stray from the path, make the choice to find your way back. You will find strength and courage in yourself along the way—do not become discouraged.

Remember the truth and light are always there, it is up to you to find your own way to pass through the stars in the universe. Remember you are not alone, for we are here to guide you along the way. (Asmuth)

Can we find "the essence of one" while on the earth plane?

Remember that "the essence of one" just "is." You can not find it in a person, place, or thing. Do you wish for me to draw you a map? Even if I did, the map would only lead you to yourself. For in you is where "the essence of one" resides. The question is, are you ready and willing to go within yourself? "The essence of one" is in your soul. When you become one with your soul, you will truly be one. I will not need to tell you that you have reached this plateau (of oneness), you will know. Knowledge and wisdom will assist you as you make the journey toward the truth and light. The journey may seem endless but then "the essence of one" is endless, isn't it?

Remember that "one" is timeless and limitless. It is a state of being devoid of size and shape. If you asked me to define "one," I could only give you a vision of light, love, and truth.

And so you ask, can you find "the essence of one" on the earth plane? The answer is that you can find oneness in your life on various levels. If you achieve oneness on every level of your life (here on the earth plane or beyond), then you may transcend to "the essence of one." When you have reached this point, you will no longer question life for you will be one with all that is, has been, and ever will be. (Shamani)

How long does it take to reach "the essence of one"?

Remember, "the essence of one" is devoid of time and space. Think of "the essence of one" as being in an elevated state beyond your body, mind, and spirit, and liken it to being way beyond yourself yet a part of yourself at the same time. Oneness on all levels of your being. You are like a smooth flowing river of consciousness. You have all the knowledge and wisdom of the universe and you are the essence of all that is, all that ever was, and all that ever will be.

When you have reached "the essence of one," you will be neither happy nor sad, you will just "be." Think of being totally surrounded by love and peace, then elevate your consciousness beyond this. You will see that you are the embodiment of love and peace.

The rate at which your soul learns its lessons is a function of your soul's choices. If you choose easy lessons, you may spend more lifetimes on the earth plane than say someone who chooses difficult lessons. Remember, whether by easy or difficult lessons, you will eventually reach "the essence of one."

If you can learn to accept the lessons you have chosen, you will see that you are the director of your life. Accept your role and focus on what you need to learn today. When you have attained oneness in your everyday life, then you will have reached "the essence of one." How long it takes to reach this point depends on how long you choose to remain separate from yourself and all other things. (Asmuth)

Conclusion

Chapter 14:

Where Do We Go From Here?

The wisdom of the ages has been bestowed upon you. Where did all life begin and where will it end? When did all life begin and when will it end? And finally, why did all life begin and why will it end? These are the questions handed down to you through time and space. The answers lie between the pages of your fingers, and indeed the answers lie within you.

Fear is the great provocator, it can unleash the best or worst in you. Yet, if you can balance courage and fear, and embrace both equally, you can be courageously fearful. This may be an oxymoron of sorts, but there is profound wisdom and truth in what I say.

Let the magic of love penetrate the thick wall of insecurity that surrounds you. Face your life challenges, do not see challenges or lessons as punishment from a higher power. For if you embrace your challenges and lessons, you will see that your potential for growth is unlimited. Love and respect yourself and others. Every soul has the potential to give and receive unlimited love.

Life on Earth and beyond is all about choices, what choices have you made? Are you happy with your choices? Life is not a random set of events. There exists a framework, based on love, which you must live in. Think about who and what you are. Essentially, you are a being of light. What you think and feel forms the base of who you truly are. You can erect barriers to keep others from discovering the truth, but you can't hide the truth from yourself.

Surely, you have more questions about life on Earth and beyond. Be patient and take the time to re-read this book. And this time, read between the lines, take a sentence, verse, paragraph, chapter, or the entire book, and apply the truth to your life. You will be forever enriched with knowledge and wisdom. You will become aware of that which has kept you from discovering who you truly are—a being filled with love, light, and truth. Till our paths cross again, may your life journey be a positive expression of who you are. I love you all, this day and always. (Asmuth)

What have we learned in the last 2000 years?

If you are bent on finding the truth, then the truth you shall find. If you are bent on finding falsity, then falsity is what you will find. The choice is simple. Indeed, you can find truth in everything, but the question is, can the truth that you have found stand in the light? Now, it is up to each of you to put your idea or concept of the truth to this test. If you are surprised at the results, then surely you have found the truth. The results may surprise those of you who thought you had found the truth, as well as those of you who thought you had not found the truth.

The last 2000 years were merely a blink in the eye of the universe. However, on the earth plane, these years have been a course in human evolution. See how your civilizations have advanced and declined. Empires based on one ego and forced on many. Advance and decline, this seems to be the path chosen by many. War and peace works on the same principle. Now I ask you, has your civilization advanced any further than those before you? Have you learned from the lessons of the past or do you continue to challenge the results of those lessons? Are your lessons characterized with disbelief?

Belief in yourself and a world beyond the earth plane is what many of you have learned in the last 2000 years. Many of you have been reincarnated many times during this period. So ask yourself, what have I learned in my soul's evolution? Have I learned to love myself and others or do I disregard love and embrace ego in order to disgrace myself? Indeed, this may be a difficult question for you to answer.

During the last 2000 years, technology, as you call it, has made numerous advances. You have learned how to sustain more life on the earth plane by sharing the technology. This is the key to your individual and collective survival on the earth plane and beyond. Greed and selfishness leaves huge gaping holes in your soul. Love is the greatest healer of all, but do you have enough love inside you to fill the holes?

In the last 2000 years, we have learned a great many things about ourselves. We have increased our knowledge and wisdom tenfold. Now the time has come to use that knowledge and wisdom to help each other. We must learn to wholeheartedly love and respect all things, "living" and "non-living." Can we learn to raise our levels of consciousness to even higher levels?

Your life can be viewed as a series of karmic justices or injustices. The responsibility for the advancement of your life lies with you. No one else can be held responsible for what you have failed to learn. It is time for each of you to step forth and take responsibility for your own life. The earth, as you know it, depends on you and you depend on it. (Shamani)

Why do we look to the past for answers?

Your past holds the keys to your present and future. Can you deny that you have learned nothing from the past? Who and what you are now is a function of your past history. Think of a book of history, do you not look for answers in this book? So why should your life be any different? If I told you your present and future are a reflection of your past, would you believe me?

One of the reasons you look to the past for answers is to confirm and verify your present experiences, feelings, ideas, and thoughts. Think of the past as a qualifier for the present. As you expand your consciousness, you will continuously look forward and backward alternately while keeping a forward direction. You will gauge your experiences of the present and compare them to the past. You will develop your own guidebook to life based on what you see as the truth. Your truth is no more and no less important than someone else's truth. You are both on a path of self-discovery and will eventually arrive at the same level of understanding.

Use the knowledge and wisdom passed down from those before you. Also, use the knowledge and wisdom that you have attained in past lives. You have a foundation on which to build the present and future. The answers you seek are those based on the truth. The journey may be long and arduous, but if you look to the past for answers, surely you will find the future. For simply, the present is the balancing point between the past and future. If you remember this, you will always be exactly where you need to be, in the present. (Asmuth)

What are the most important global concerns at this time?

You—citizens of the universe—must unite. What you do globally will have universal effects. The unification of all souls on earth for a common purpose. Harmony is essential to life as you know it. Without harmony, the fragments of beings float in the ethos (ethers).

War must be aborted. The senseless maniacal killing must be no more. Power, greed, jealousy, and hate can not be left unabated.

Destruction of the forests can not continue. Deforestation for profit serves the needs of the few.

Mass consumption is another global concern. Many of you have your minds set on accumulating resources without using them properly. Your life can not be measured by how much you have.

Self-centeredness and selfishness are other global concerns. I often hear what's mine is mine and not yours. Can such ideas sustain a planet?

Another concern is the wasting of resources. You only use what you need or desire and throw the rest away. Do you stop to think that someone else may be able to use that which you throw away?

Another concern is space and the way you use it. I speak of the land and the oceans. I hear you ask, where have all the flowers gone? I reply, you have planted grass and concrete over the flowers. Your idea of beauty has replaced the natural beauty. Use your space more wisely. It is sad to see that you need preservations and reservations. You create places where natural beauty is preserved.

I say to you, all of these concerns are important. There are many other concerns. It is up to you, as citizens of the universe, to unify on a global level. Love yourself and love the earth. By doing this, all things are possible. (Asmuth)

What global direction would most benefit our growth?

Individually and globally, you should always move forward, closer to the light and truth. In order to keep this forward motion, you must embrace both love and peace. Mere words of love or peace mean little unless they are spoken from the heart. It is far easier to say you want love and peace in the world, and far more difficult to practice them in your daily life.

Earth is a learning ground for each of you. What you learn on Earth will propel you forward to new dimensions of truth. The knowledge and wisdom you attain in this incarnation will benefit your growth as well as others' growth. Together, each of you make a contribution to the universal consciousness. Your acts of love and peace benefit everything universally. Remember, the universe does not revolve around you. So I ask each and every one of you to be more patient with each other. If you expect less, you will receive more.

Knowledge and wisdom, love and peace, care and respect, and light and truth—these are the universal laws by which you may choose to live. Individually and globally, you can choose to direct or redirect your life for the benefit of all. The direction you take will always propel you to new levels of awareness and growth. And once you become aware, you must always maintain a forward motion.

Collectively, you have the potential to create a world based on eternal love and peace. Again, the profession of words alone means little unless spoken from the heart. So I ask you, are words of love and peace spoken from your heart? Although it may seem you are only one heart and one voice, the words you speak can have global implications. If you can attain love and peace globally, then the light and the truth will be illuminated universally. (Shamani)

What lies in what we call Outer Space?

Life, full of dimensions, cryptic messages, messages carried far. Physical dimensions, peaceful, serenity. Cataclysmic universe—oh sacred one, dimension without form. Thoughts carried along waves—waves of intent, wisdom personified, the endless spectrum. However, at the center, all which life revolves around. The revolution of time. Time. Endless time. The universe stagnant. The stars, stories to be told of life as we know it, devoid of reason. The best kept secrets, secrets once told but now revealed.

Space, frontiers of fantasy and fallacy—what direction do we take? Blasphemous desires, caverns of ideas, discoveries foretold, human tendencies from whence we first came. In search of life, formless, devoid of spirit. Yet spirit forms the center, the ecliptic union of souls. Blessed is the place from whence we came. Now, we seek a way back—a way to the light, the light of the spirit.

I find the way difficult myself at times, but with reason and purpose, the way becomes well lit. The oppressed seek to find a way out of the bloodless heart, the truth of the ideas put forth before us. The ideas reign supreme.

Envisioning new life, a new way, a new path. A journey to another plane. A planeless dimension, one without surface (without a bottom). But you would think you would fall through. Fall through to what, support comes through thought. Think it is there and it will be.

Glasses to see with, false security for those who need it. I say, shed those glasses and look forward. Space, all around us, what do you see? Does it take form? Does it have rhyme or reason? Magical and mystical, a tendency toward the abyss—the great catacomb of life. Life without space would be life without time. Who can say if space is real at all or imagined. It is what you make it. Create space between yourselves. A space we call home, but does it really exist? Yes, if only in our minds. Minds are the wanderers, the purists, the destined. Minds devoid of space and time. A place I call home. (Asmuth)

Do you have any predictions for the year 2000?

Does your concept of time, a new millennium, warrant predictions? Again, so many of you seem controlled by a number. The "time" has come for many of you to realize that the ways of the past will not work in the near future.

You are entering a space where much of what you have accepted as truth is being challenged. As I said, you are seeing that the old thoughts and ideas, based on false power and security, are not working. We who reside beyond the earth plane have seen all of this develop and unfold. Many of you seek revenge and retribution against each other for untold offenses. There are many among you who seek to control others through greed. I see cycles of hatred and anger being perpetuated worldwide. So you ask, can the end of the world be near? Is there any hope? Will negativity prevail?

So you say, you want predictions. Based on what I've previously said, it would seem that many of you would expect predictions of worldwide devastation. Although there is seemingly a lot of negative energy being perpetuated, there is hope. The hope is strong and lives in the souls of all of you who inhabit the earth plane.

I predict that the walls of insecurity and inadequacy will fall. Those who seek to control others will meet their own demise. All of you will be called upon to look within yourselves and bring out the love to share with all things of creation. The year 2000 will be a "time" of consciousness-raising. There will be those who choose to participate and those who choose not to participate. Regardless, the wheels of progress have been set into motion. In order for many of you to survive on the earth plane, the collective consciousness must be elevated. The time has come. The question is, will you accept or reject elevated consciousness?

I do not see physical devastation of the earth, as many of you predict. I do believe that many of you have seen the light at the end of the tunnel, and have taken it upon yourself to start elevating your consciousness in anticipation of what lies ahead. Remember that each of you is responsible for what happens in the year 2000. The question is, will you be ready to accept what has been written by you? Are you a prophet of doom or truth—let your consciousness decide! (Asmuth)

What will be the lessons of the year 2000?

Many of you await the coming of the year 2000. You either see it as a symbol of hope or as the end of the world. The year 2000 is merely a date in time created by those who walked the earth before you. If you place your entire fate in one year, then you may see exactly what you have come to believe.

It is true that the year 2000 on the earth plane is a breaking point between so-called millenniums. You are faced with many choices and decisions. Who can better make an individual choice or decision than you? You are the ruler of your destiny. Are you ready to place your destiny in the hands of others? Or will you rise up and stand tall in the presence of soothsayers, false prophets, and false predictors?

Time is inversely proportional to the way you live. When you attempt to control time, you see that you are controlled by it. Control is one of the most important lessons of the year 2000. It is important for you to learn that control and power are required tools for those weak in spirit. If you choose to control others or seek power over them, then you will see that you have no control or power over yourself.

Fortresses which you build around yourself can be easily toppled. Let the new millennium be a personal symbol of hope for you. Hope is often derived from feelings of hopelessness. So many of you feel that the earth has taken an irreversible course toward destruction and disaster. I say to you, it is never too late to chart a new path. If you choose a new path, remain focused on positive actions and changes. Love is the eternal savior.

Another lesson of the year 2000 is to learn how to properly utilize the computer technology you possess. The key to this is the word "possession." For when you possess something, you hide it from others. What are you afraid of? Do you think others are not capable of such ego-based centricism? The technology you have been given—you have not begun to understand how it works. You are only concerned with the speed at which it works. Has it made your life less complicated or has it had the opposite effect? And what about those people in other "impoverished" countries who do not "possess" this technology? Are they the forgotten souls?

Remember earlier in this century, when automobiles were first introduced. Now, ninety years later, are there still not people that can not afford such luxuries? Why is this, you ask? Well, the technology was possessed by a few instead of shared. Until each of you learns to share all things, especially love, it will always seem like there is pain and suffering in the world.

As you prepare yourself for entry into a new millennium, remember what I have said. Many of you will not see the light of day in the year 2000, but do not worry for the light still shines upon you. Your life on the earth plane is just as important as your life beyond. Learn to love and respect one another, regardless of what time it is. This is the lesson of truth which I bestow upon you. Now go and spread the truth. (Asmuth)

What were the lessons of the 2000s (2000–2010)?

You who sit idly by the fire, await the trial by fire. As I look to a time period which has occurred already, but which you have yet to experience, I see widespread devastation and famine, nuclear holocaust, the land in ruins. And all because those who had the foresight did not use it to warn others. The warnings were not heeded. But alas miracles do happen, you have been spared this prophetic injustice. But just think if all I said would have happened. Would you change your life path now or would you continue onward and upward?

Ladders are only as strong as the person who uses them. The steps of the ladder are symbols of every major step in your life. If you try to take two steps at a time, you will miss the step in between. And that step which you avoided may be the difference between life and death.

The lessons you have chosen for the years 2000–2010 are etched in stone. Are you ready to accept what you have chosen? Change does not come easily to those who resist it. For many of you, resistance is a way of life. Resist what you do not understand and covet what you do understand. Take the first step toward making your life better today. Tomorrow is just a phone call away. Who will you call to rescue you from drowning in your own sorrow?

Take what you have learned today and project it five to ten years into the future. If you do, you will surely see the lessons of the years 2000–2010 illuminated before you. Charlatans and prophets can predict future events only because they see it with their own eyes. You can choose to see and hear what you want to see and hear.

The lessons of the years 2000–2010 are but a memory for me but for you they have yet to begin. You can choose the path least traveled or most traveled. But when you reach the end of the path, you will see that you are exactly where you need to be, here and now. For here and now is what is truly important. (Shamani)

How can we find happiness and peace?

Align your mind, body, and spirit with all that is. I speak of universal everlasting happiness and peace.

Many of you find temporary happiness and peace in your life. But does it ever seem to last? Look at the birds in the sky, they seem so happy and peaceful. The birds allow their spirits to soar high above/atop the land. What is their secret of flight? The birds freely express their spirit, they believe that the wind will carry their spirit.

And so you must allow your spirit to soar. Do not be afraid of the freedom. For in the freedom, you will find peace and happiness. But you ask, how can I find peace and happiness every day and once I find it, how can I hold onto it? The answers lie within you. Do not look to material possessions for happiness and peace. Possessions are disguises of happiness and peace. The happiness and peace you feel soon fades into memory, then you are left seeking happiness and peace again.

In order to find lasting feelings of happiness and peace, you must embrace love. Love is all that is. Build a foundation of love, affirm your right to happiness and peace. Happiness and peace is abundant in you, you have the keys. It is up to you to unlock the floodgates. Remember, you must be prepared to accept what you ask for.

You can not possess happiness and peace. If you try to, you will find it is ever elusive. I ask you to take a good look at yourself, evaluate your life, and ask yourself what would make you truly happy. Once you have done this, then make happiness your personal goal. Remain focused on your goal. Release yourself from your past and focus on the present moment. Let your spirit soar for peace awaits you. (Shamani)

How can we find home?

The sunlight glistens through the leaves. The leaves of gold shine upon you. You are home.

The place you seek can be ever elusive. Many of you feel that once you live in a certain place, buy something that makes you happy, or marry someone and buy a house, then you will have a home. This may be true, but it is only a temporary substitute for happiness.

When you find true happiness, you will be home.

It is important for you (while you are on the earth plane) to find a place which provides comfort and security. Some of you find it with another person, in a house, or possibly in nature. Nurture the feelings of comfort and security, learn to recognize them. By doing this, you perpetuate love for your soul.

Home is not a place, thing, or space in time. It is a state of being—oneness. When you have achieved oneness, you will truly be home. (Shamani)

About the Authors

Alan Fass, a celestial communicator, interacts with numerous spirit guides/angels on a daily basis. He has spent the last eleven years meditating, studying, and listening to these voices of the universe. For the last five years, he has been "conversing" with his spirit guides/angels and others who have made the journey beyond this plane. For the first time, in *Answers From Above,* he offers his angels' messages of love, peace, and hope to all who wish to receive them.

Alan, also a professional geologist and environmental consultant, has worked tirelessly to help return the earth to its natural state. His daily life reflects the principles outlined in Asmuth and Shamani's messages. He recently realized his lifelong dream of finding an older home in the mountains to "recycle" and then he rebuilt it for his family.

Pamela Fass, a writer, editor, and former public speaking and business communication instructor, has spent most of her life trying to foster communication between and amongst all types of people. While earning degrees in psychology and communication, and a Certificate in Women's Studies, she spent her "free time" organizing multicultural and women-centered events and working to promote awareness of human, animal, and environmental rights issues. A semi-vegetarian for thirteen years and a complete vegetarian for eleven years, as well as a student of metaphysical literature, she has always been interested in the mind/body/spirit connection.

Alan and Pamela Fass live together in the Appalachian Mountains of Tennessee, with the trees, animals, and local country folk as their neighbors. They plan to spend the rest of their lives loving each other, working to create a better world for all of our children, and asking the questions that need to be answered.

Index

Answers From Above
Order Form

Please send ___ copies of *Answers From Above* to:

Name: ______________________________________
(Please print)

Address: ______________________________________

City, State, Zip Code: ______________________________

Telephone: ______________ E-mail: __________________

(Telephone numbers and e-mail addresses are used only if there is a question about your order.)

Please send $14.95 for each copy plus $2.95 shipping* to:

Aseer Publishing
P.O. Box 188
Washburn, TN 37888

Tennessee residents add 8.75% sales tax ($1.31 per book).

*Add $1.95 shipping for each additional book sent to the same address.

I would like to see these topics addressed in upcoming *Answers* books:

____

____

____

____

Answers From Above
Gift Order Form

Please send _ copies of *Answers From Above* to:

Name: ____

(Please print)

Address: ______________________________________

City, State, Zip Code: ______________________________

Telephone: ________________ E-mail: ____________________

(Telephone numbers and e-mail addresses are used only if there is a question about your order.)

Please send $14.95 for each copy plus $2.95 shipping* to:

Aseer Publishing
P.O. Box 188
Washburn, TN 37888

Tennessee residents add 8.75% sales tax ($1.31 per book).

*Add $1.95 shipping for each additional book sent to the same address.

____

Please enclose this note with my gift:

____

____

____

____

(Please Print)